The Workplace

The Workplace
TODAY AND TOMORROW

Dr. Joe Pace

Boston   Burr Ridge, IL   Dubuque, IA   Madison, WI   New York   San Francisco   St. Louis
Bangkok   Bogotá   Caracas   Kuala Lumpur   Lisbon   London   Madrid   Mexico City
Milan   Montreal   New Delhi   Santiago   Seoul   Singapore   Sydney   Taipei   Toronto

The McGraw·Hill Companies

Mc Graw Hill **Higher Education**

THE PROFESSIONAL DEVELOPMENT SERIES: BOOK ONE: THE WORKPLACE: TODAY AND TOMORROW
Published by McGraw-Hill, a business unit of The McGraw-Hill Companies, Inc., 1221
Avenue of the Americas, New York, NY, 10020. Copyright (2006 by The McGraw-Hill
Companies, Inc. All rights reserved. No part of this publication may be reproduced or
distributed in any form or by any means, or stored in a database or retrieval system, without
the prior written consent of The McGraw-Hill Companies, Inc., including, but not limited to,
in any network or other electronic storage or transmission, or broadcast for distance learning.
Some ancillaries, including electronic and print components, may not be available to
customers outside the United States.

This book is printed on acid-free paper.

0 ROV 15 14 13 12 11

ISBN: 978-0-07-860570-3
MHID: 0-07-860570-9

Publisher: *Emily Barrosse*
Executive editor: *David S. Patterson*
Developmental editor: *Anne Sachs*
Senior marketing manager: *Leslie Oberhuber*
Senior media producer: *Todd Vaccaro*
Project manager: *Jean R. Starr*
Production supervisor: *Janean A. Utley*
Associate designer: *Srdjan Savanovic*
Media project manager: *Marc Mattson*
Photo research coordinator: *Natalia C. Peschiera*
Art editor: *Ayelet Arbel*
Photo researcher: *Natalia Peschiera*
Art director: *Jeanne Schreiber*
Cover design: *Srdjan Savanovic*
Cover photo: *© Corbis.com*
Interior design: *Kiera Pohl*
Typeface: *9.5/12 Palatino*
Compositor: *Carlisle Communications, Ltd.*
Printer: *R.R. Donnelley and Sons Inc.*

www.mhhe.com

Contents

As a psychologist and former college president involved in higher education for over thirty-six years, I often have been asked what skills most directly contribute to career success.

The questioner generally expects me to talk about job skills. Thirty years ago, it would have been typing. Today, it might be familiarity with common workplace software.

But the fact is that most employers don't care how fast you type or how well you align columns on a spreadsheet.

What Do Employers Want?

In a recent survey,* business owners and corporate executives in the United States were asked to rate what they valued most in a new employee:

- Dependability—35%
- Honesty—27%
- Good attitude—19%
- Competence—19%

What does this tell us? It says, simply, that 81 percent of corporations in the United States rate the personal qualities of dependability, honesty, and attitude—what I call *professionalism*—above any skills-based competencies.

The Need for *Professionalism*

Does it make sense that employers value professionalism over what we generally think of as job-related skills? Certainly. All jobs and businesses are different. Even companies manufacturing similar products in the same city will have their own unique procedures and policies. Working for one does not mean you can easily transition into working for another. Employers know this. They know that they will have to train you in the skills necessary for your job and they are willing to do this. What employers want from you are the internal qualities that make you trainable.

Employers want you to be reliable; they want you to be hardworking; and they want you to be ethical. In a word, employers look for the qualities that make a person *professional*.

Padgett Business Services, quarterly survey of service and retail clients.

Why *The Professional Development Series?*

The sad fact is that most colleges and schools spend an overwhelming majority of the time and energy developing hard skills while ignoring the personal qualities of character and dependability that actually get people hired. The good news is that—like typing or programming—professionalism can be taught.

My aim in developing this *Professional Development Series* has been to teach the personal skills that lead to job and career success. The *Series* is based on both my own research on career success and my experience as a lecturer, college president, and mentor. The material I present in the *Series* is the same material I have used to guide thousands of students and to train hundreds of instructors across North America. The goal for teachers who use the *Series* is to help turn out graduates ready to meet the challenges of the fast-paced professional world. The goal for students learning with the *Series* is to succeed in their chosen careers and, more importantly, to succeed in life.

The Books in *The Professional Development Series*

The Professional Development Series is easy to read and user-friendly. The books are brief, because you are busy. The books are practical, because you need specific guidance, not vague assurances. Each book and every chapter use a consistent organization of text and features to structure the material.

Book 1: The Workplace: Today and Tomorrow

Book One is an orientation to the world of work. In it, you will consider the occupations that are most likely to have job openings in the coming years, how to prepare yourself to fill these openings, and what the workplace environment is like in the twenty-first century. Professional business protocol, professional presence, and a customer-first attitude also are explored and discussed.

Book 2: The Workplace: Interpersonal Strengths and Leadership

Professional success in the twenty-first century demands that people work together to achieve their goals. Book 2: *Interpersonal Strengths and Leadership* explores and develops the skills that make a person a good teammate and a good leader. Developing a standard of excellence and pride in your work along with understanding ethics, trust, and respect also is covered. Thinking strategically and modeling leadership techniques are addressed as well.

Book 3: The Workplace: Personal Skills for Success

Time management and stress management come to mind when we talk about *Personal Skills for Success* and in Book 3, you will develop and practice these skills. You also will be encouraged to think about who you are and what you believe and to use what you learn to establish goals for the future and to develop a plan to achieve those goals. Communicating and presenting ideas and concepts, as well as thinking critically and creatively, also are covered.

Book 4: The Workplace: Chart Your Career

One day you leave school and you have a job; twenty years later you look back and realize that you have a career. How can you make sure that the career you have is fulfilling and rewarding? How can you avoid or overcome the inevitable missteps—taking the wrong job, for example—and get your career back on track? Book 4 offers guidance on planning a career and, more importantly, on developing, changing, and maintaining it.

Features of Each Book in *The Professional Development Series*

Every chapter of each book has a consistent format, clearly organizing the material to help you learn.

Beginning Each Chapter

What Will You Do? The entire plan for the chapter is set out in What Will You Do? Each section within the chapter is called out with a one-sentence summary describing the content.

Why Do You Need to Know This? The information in each chapter is there for a reason. Why Do You Need to Know This? explains how the material will be useful in finding a job, building a rewarding career, or succeeding in life.

Set the Pace Before beginning a chapter, it is important to determine what you already know about the topic. Set the Pace asks you to think about your own experiences with the subject.

Objectives These are your goals for the chapter. When you have done the reading and the work for each chapter, you should have learned about and practiced each of the bulleted skills. These Objectives will be revisited in the Chapter Summary.

Beginning Each Section

Reading and Study Tip Each tip presents a helpful suggestion to aid your retention of the material in the section.

In Each Section

Quotations These thoughts offer inspiration, context, and perspective from important and influential people in all walks of life.

Vocabulary Important terms are called out in the margins and defined.

New Attitudes/New Opportunities These profiles present real people giving voice to their real-world goals, concerns, and experiences.

Pace Points Techniques and advice that I have found useful from my own work experience.

Judgment Call These real-world scenarios call on you to interpret and act on the information in the section. Check your answers online at www.mhhe.com/pace.

Dr. Joe Pace These are quotations from my workshops that, over time, my students have found the most meaningful.

Ending Each Section

Quick Recap Here is a summary to help you review the section material, check yourself with short review questions, and check your answers online at www.mhhe.com/pace.

Chapter Review and Activities

Chapter Summary The chapter's Objectives reappear here with a review of what you should know about each section and about each objective.

Business Vocabulary All the vocabulary terms from the chapter are listed with the page number where they can be found within the chapter. Double-check to make sure you know what each word means and how it is used.

Key Concept Review Short-answer questions in the Key Concept Review will help you remember the material from each section.

Online Project Go online to learn more about what you have learned in the chapter.

Step Up the Pace These real-world scenarios help you think about applying what you have learned in the chapter to your own life, job, and career.

Business Skills Brush-Up This activity gives you the chance to practice important business skills such as critical reading and effective writing.

Support for *The Professional Development Series*

The books of the *Series* are supported by

Professional Development Series **website (www.mhhe.com/pace)** On the website, students can find answers to questions posed in the text, additional chapter review materials, and topics for additional reading and study. Instructors also can access sample syllabi, suggested test questions, and tips for teaching.

Study Smart **Study Skills Tutorial** From time management to taking notes, *Study Smart* is an excellent way to practice your skills. *Study Smart* was developed by Andrea Bonner and Mieke Schipper of Sir Sanford Fleming College and is available on CD-ROM (0–07–245515–2). This innovative study skills tutorial teaches students essential note-taking methods, test-taking strategies, and time management secrets. *Study Smart* is free when packaged with the books of *The Professional Development Series*.

BusinessWeek Online Interested instructors can offer their students 15 weeks of access to *BusinessWeek* Online by requesting that a password card be packaged with the books of *The*

Professional Development Series. For further information call 1–800–338–3987 or speak to your McGraw-Hill Sales Representative.

Instructor's Resource CD-ROM This is a thorough guide to planning, organizing, and administering courses using *The Professional Development Series*. The CD includes sample syllabi, model assessments, and test questions, and teaching tips for each section in every chapter of all four books.

About the Author

For over thirty-six years, Dr. Joe Pace has been a nationally recognized speaker, author, and educator. A psychologist and former college president, Dr. Pace currently serves as the managing partner of the Education Initiative for The Pacific Institute.

Dr. Pace is creator of the *Success Strategies for Effective Colleges and Schools* program implemented worldwide in over 200 colleges and schools. He has served as commissioner of the Accrediting Council of Independent Colleges and Schools (ACICS) in Washington, D.C.; on the board of directors of The Association of Independent Colleges and Schools, now known as the CCA (Career College Association); and as president of the Florida Association of Postsecondary Schools and Colleges.

A popular keynote speaker at conferences and conventions, Dr. Pace also has conducted a variety of seminars and workshops throughout North America on such topics as school management, faculty development, student retention, psychology, and motivation. Thousands of college-level students have benefited from his expertise in the areas of psychology, personal development, and business administration.

Dr. Pace is known for his warmth, enthusiasm, humor, and "intelligent heart." His audiences enjoy his genuine spirit and heartwarming stories. Because of his loving and caring nature, Dr. Pace is able to help people to succeed in their chosen careers, but more importantly, to succeed in life.

Acknowledgments

The energy to develop this series has come from my family: my wife Sharon, my daughters Tami and Tiffany, my son-in-law John, and my grandkids Nicholas, Jessica, Dylan, and Jonathan. Their love and support get me up in the morning, inspire my work, and excite me about tomorrow.

Thanks also to Shawn Knieriem, my director of operations, for her assistance and support with this project.

My special thanks to the Advisory Board and Review Panel for their excellent suggestions, tips, techniques, and wisdom, as well as for their time and effort in attending various meetings. I have considered them friends and colleagues for many years and it was an honor to work with them on this project.

Advisory Board In October of 2002, a group of educators came together to chart the course for the project that would become *The Professional Development Series*. Their insights and vision guided me.

Teresa Beatty, ECPI

Gary Carlson, ITT Educational Services

Jerry Gallentine, National American University

Gery Hochanadel, Keiser College

Jim Howard, Sanford Brown Colleges

Ken Konesco, Indiana Business Colleges

Review Panel Once the Board provided the goal, the Review Panel undertook to develop the project. Their sage advice influenced every page of *The Professional Development Series*.

Steve Calabro, Southwest Florida College

JoAnna Downey, Corinthian Colleges

Barb Gillespie, Cuyamaca College

Lynn Judy, Carteret Community College

Ken Konesco, Indiana Business Colleges

Ada Malcioln, International Institute of the Americas

Dena Montiel, Santa Ana School of Continuing Education

Peggy Patlan, Fox College

Sharon Roseman, Computer Career Center

Peggy Schlechter, National American University

The Workplace

Understand Tomorrow's Job Opportunities

What Will You Do?

1.1 Career Directions Look at the many directions a career can take and understand the importance of developing transferable skills during your professional growth.

1.2 Information Technology Examine some of the jobs in the country's fastest-growing industry and understand the importance of continuously upgrading your skills to keep up with technology.

1.3 Health Science Learn about the potential rewards of a job in the health sciences.

1.4 Retail/Wholesale Sales and Service Recognize the jobs involved in bringing products from the manufacturing plant to the hands of the final customer.

1.5 Communication and Media Examine a career cluster that includes both the technicians that make modern communication and media work and the creative people who provide information and entertainment to the public.

1.6 Finance and Accounting Assess the finance and accounting career cluster and understand how the management, measurement, movement, and recording of transactions can put professionals into the highest levels of management.

Why Do You Need to Know This?

The world has never offered so many career opportunities. Today's professionals can choose to go in directions that stimulate their interests, challenge their capabilities, and provide the income they need for the lifestyle they deserve. With so many choices, it's easy to go astray. Your career will last most of the rest of your life. By choosing the right career today, you can more quickly achieve your personal and professional goals. However, choosing the "wrong" career isn't necessarily a personal or professional disaster. By continuing your education throughout your career, you can prepare yourself to shift directions as your interests change.

Chapter Objectives

After completing this chapter, you will be able to:

- Understand the careers that five business fields offer professionals.

- Assess trends and job prospects in five business areas.

- Appreciate the skills necessary to succeed in various career tracks.

- Identify regions where each of the five industries is strongest.

Set the *Pace*

Understand Tomorrow's Job Opportunities You want a satisfying career, one that's interesting, challenging, and secure and pays the salary you need to live the way you want to live. Write a few sentences in response to each of the following questions:

- In what kind of environment do you see yourself working?
- What kind of people would you like to work with?
- What skills and knowledge are you willing to pursue?

Activity Think of the jobs your friends, family members, or even fictional television or movie characters hold. Do you aspire to have a job like theirs? Write a paragraph about your "dream job."

Career Directions

Your career choices are as wide as the world. You can apply yourself to science. You can help people in medicine or social work. You can challenge yourself in the people-to-people field of retail sales or put yourself into the high-powered field of accounting and finance. You also can channel your creative energies into communication and media.

Where Do You Want to Go? You have the rest of your life to pursue a career, but the choices start right now. This chapter will present those choices and take you on a quick tour of a few industries that offer a bright future.

Reading and Study Tip

Topic Sentences
Most paragraphs begin with a topic sentence stating the main idea of the paragraph. Find at least two paragraphs in this section that begin with a topic sentence.

Transferable Skills

Start by giving some thought to developing skills that will help you adapt to change when it comes. If you go into information technology (IT), for example, you'll be able to work in the IT part of the medical industry, the retail industry, and many others. All use computer systems, so as long as you can adapt to the special requirements of different fields, you can shift jobs without learning a whole new set of skills.

The transferable skills that bridge your shift from one industry to another are the same skills you learned in high school:

- Speaking
- Writing
- Organizing
- Interacting with other people
- Basic computer skills

You can take these skills with you wherever your career may go. With these general skills and your main area of expertise, you can shift your career as you move ahead.

Continuing Education

continuing education education and training pursued after graduation for the sake of better professional performance

Most good careers will require continuing education. **Continuing education** is training that you pursue after graduation for the sake of better professional performance. The education you receive before your first big job will get you started, but then the real learning begins. As you see the many options that your career field offers, you'll be looking for opportunities in various specialties. You'll have a lot to keep up with, including

- Changes in technology.
- New products that you either use or sell.
- Changes in legal requirements relating to environment, labor, financial reporting, and so forth.
- Developments in techniques, industry standards, markets, and so on.

Tips From a Mentor

Ten Things to Do When Looking for a Job

- *Involve family and friends* by asking for useful contacts. Networking is one of the most productive activities of any job search!

- *Ask three people to review your résumé* and give you comments.

- *Explore your options!* Never say no to an opportunity. Even if the job isn't for you, looking into it may lead to one that is!

- *Consider using a headhunter.* Recruitment specialists often have inside information or contacts. They can be especially helpful if you are in a new place with few contacts of your own.

- *Accept temporary work or even volunteer* in the company or industry you'd like to join. Temporary and volunteer work often lead to permanent job offers.

- *Role-play interviewing.* Have a friend play the role of the interviewer. Even interviewing yourself with a mirror will be good practice.

- *Research the industry.* Know the major companies, trends, salaries, and whatever else you can find out. Your research will prepare you not only for the interview, but also for the job itself.

- *Take classes* or seminars to update your knowledge and skills. However, make sure not to over qualify yourself for the job you want.

- *Research the company.* Find out the company's products or services, chief executives, locations, and basic policies and the person who does the hiring.

- *Treat your job search like a job.* Keep at it—the payoff will be worth it!

Educational Opportunities

As you immerse yourself in your new profession, you'll find educational opportunities all around you, such as

- Colleges and universities that offer continuing education courses.
- **Trade associations,** whose missions often include improving professional standards in a given industry or profession by offering conferences and seminars.
- In-house training, offered by your company.
- Trade magazines to help you keep up with what's happening in your industry, from technology to market conditions.
- Vendors who provide products that your industry uses or sells and provide seminars that explain the use of their products.

trade associations organizations dedicated to improving professional standards in a given industry or profession

Dr. Joe Pace
DETERMINATION

"The race is not always to the swift...but to those who keep running!"

" When you have a dream you've got to grab it and never let go. "

Carol Burnett
Entertainer

- The Internet with all sorts of online courses, many of them provided by colleges, universities, private professional education organizations, and professional associations.
- Education packages consisting of books, CD-ROMs, reference materials, and tests that sometimes grant credit.

Remember, the only careers that advance upwards are careers that demand continuous education, and professionals with the most education tend to be the ones most likely to succeed.

Career Clusters

When you choose a career in a given industry, you'll have opportunities in a wide variety of workplaces. A career in information technology, for example, can lead you to jobs in banking, meteorology, Web site design, software development, computer assembly, training, technical writing, hospital equipment service, and many other areas. All the occupations associated with a given industry are called a *career cluster*. The occupations in a career cluster tend to demand the same fundamental training and education, though each occupation will call for its own special skills.

When you consider a career, look for the opportunities within a career cluster. Do you want to develop the skills required by those careers? Does the cluster offer you the kinds of companies, workplaces, salaries, and benefits that you want?

Career Pathways and Ladders

A career pathway is an area of concentration, or a specific direction, taken through a career cluster. Each pathway leads to a group of careers that require similar academic and technical skills, perhaps even the same certifications. For example, in the health services career cluster, you may want to take a career pathway into occupations involving patient care. Such jobs include emergency medical technician, licensed practical nurse, registered nurse, dental hygienist, and anesthesiologist.

Your career ladder is the pathway you take or intend to take toward your career objectives. See Climbing a Career Ladder, Figure 1.1, for one example. Visualize each rung of the ladder as a job that moves you upward in your career. As you plan to take a new job, consider whether it is a step upward, and whether it prepares you for the *next* step.

QUICK RECAP 1.1

CAREER DIRECTIONS

- Transferable skills (reading, writing, organizing, etc.) will help you shift between career tracks.
- A career cluster consists of all the occupations associated with a given industry.
- A career pathway is one direction that a career might take through a career cluster.
- A career ladder is the series of jobs that an individual holds as he or she advances through a career.
- Your education will be continuous throughout your career.

Figure 1.1 *Climbing a Career Ladder*

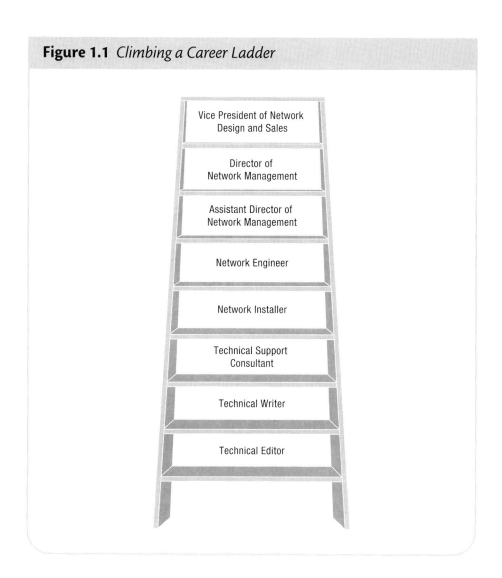

Vice President of Network Design and Sales
Director of Network Management
Assistant Director of Network Management
Network Engineer
Network Installer
Technical Support Consultant
Technical Writer
Technical Editor

CHECK YOURSELF

1. What are transferable skills and how can they help you in your career?
2. Name four sources of continuing professional education.

Check your answers online at **www.mhhe.com/pace.** *Pace* ONLINE

BUSINESS VOCABULARY

continuing education   education and training pursued after graduation for the sake of better professional performance

trade associations   organizations dedicated to improving professional standards in a given industry or profession

Information Technology

Information technology (IT) is the industry of computer hardware (physical computer equipment) and software (the applications that make computers work), including the Internet and the World Wide Web. The challenges of an IT career are great because you'll need to keep learning as fast as technology advances. However, the rewards are also great. IT careers offer many opportunities and much potential for personal and professional growth.

Take the IT Track. This section addresses the IT industry. Since IT touches just about every industry from aerospace to the arts, it offers career paths that go in all directions. Which one is right for you?

What Is Information Technology?

Information technology (IT) is used to design, develop, set up, operate, and support computer systems. The IT industry includes computer assembly, software design, networking, use of the Internet and the World Wide Web, and use of computers in all sorts of applications. Computers control hospital equipment, traffic lights, credit card payments, automatic teller machines, television studios, robots in factories, air traffic control systems, investment and financial systems—more things and functions than anyone could ever list.

In other words, information technology is everywhere, and so are IT jobs. A career in IT gives you opportunities in just about every industry in the world, including, of course, the companies that produce computer hardware and software.

The IT Workplace

IT professionals generally enjoy workplaces that have been designed for a comfortable, productive workday. Most jobs are in office buildings, usually at large and medium-sized corporations.

It is becoming increasingly common for IT professionals to work from home offices, often connecting to a corporate office by Internet. Since much of their work involves nothing more than a computer and electronic data, their physical presence in a business office is not needed. Some professionals work from a **virtual office,** connecting their laptop computers wherever they are.

virtual office a portable office, consisting mostly of a laptop computer

The IT Career Cluster

The IT career cluster can be organized into four career pathways (see Figure 1.2):

1. Information support and services
2. Programming and software development
3. Network systems
4. Interactive media

Figure 1.2 *The Information Technology Career Cluster*

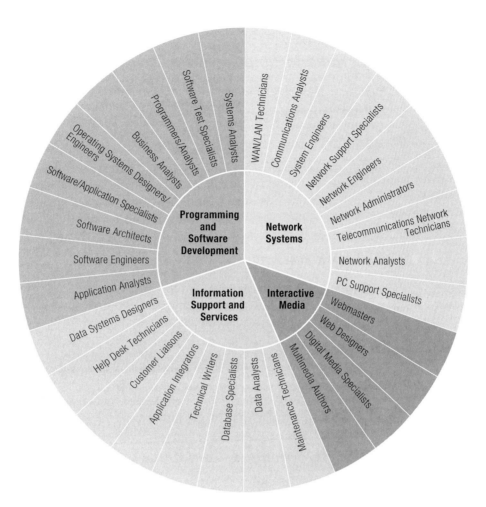

Thinking Critically IT involves the design, development, support, and management of hardware, software, multimedia, and systems integration services. *How do your skills and interests fit with jobs in the information technology cluster?*

Information Support and Services

As you can see from the information technology career cluster, information support and services employ more people than any other IT pathway. Employees must continue their education in order to keep up with advancing technology. Professionals in this field hold a wide variety of jobs. Their duties include

- Analyzing computer users' requirements.
- Selecting the best IT solution for a given set of requirements.
- Designing computer systems or software that makes the solution work.
- Implementing and operating the system.
- Teaching people how to use the system.
- Maintaining the data in the system.
- Fixing or changing the system when it breaks or needs improvement.
- Writing instruction manuals.
- Staffing technical support desks and telephone help lines.

Preparation   Skills and education levels in this career pathway vary widely. Many professionals have degrees in computer science. Many have degrees in unrelated areas but have an aptitude for IT. Some pick up their skills while holding a non-IT job. Some take courses at technical schools, at community colleges, or online.

Programming and Software Development

Professionals in programming design software and translate their designs into computer code. They know several programming languages. Their skill with logic must be very strong, their thinking must be very methodical, and they must be able to focus on detail.

Preparation   Programmers and software developers usually hold a college degree in computer science, information technology, information systems, or mathematics. Some receive enough training at technical schools or community colleges to get started on this career pathway, then they learn more as they advance.

Network Systems

network systems links among computers and peripherals that enable several people to share software, files, computers, and peripherals at the same time

Network systems link computers so that several people can share software, files, computers, and peripherals at the same time. Some networks link the computers in a single office. Others link computers all over the world. The Internet is actually a system of networks that connects hundreds of millions of users.

Preparation   People who work in network systems support must have strong technical skills in computer operation and electrical installation. A college degree may not be necessary, but extensive specialized training is. Training is often available from the producers of network software.

Interactive Media/E-Commerce

Interactive media electronic systems that allow users to input information and receive responses, as in computer games, chat rooms, and computer-based interactive training programs

E-commerce business conducted over the Internet

Interactive media are electronic systems that allow users to input information and receive responses. Computer games, chat rooms, and interactive computer-based training programs are examples of interactive media. Many Web sites are interactive, especially those that allow **e-commerce**—business conducted over the Internet.

E-commerce has been growing rapidly as companies create Web sites that allow customers to order products or seek technical assistance over the Internet. Professionals who work in this area of IT may be involved in Web page design, online payment systems, or writing of technical assistance scripts.

Preparation   Professionals in e-commerce need to use many programming languages. Education often includes a degree in business or marketing, with strong training in computer graphics and programming languages.

Jobs in IT

Information technology embraces dozens of job titles and all levels of education and skill (Figure 1.3). Here are a few of the more common jobs, and the qualifications required to do them:

- **Computer Engineer** Hardware computer engineers design and develop computers, components, and peripherals. Software engineers design software, a complex process of determining how data should flow through a computer. Software engineers write computer code to make the software work.

Figure 1.3 *Sample Career Ladders in Information Technology*

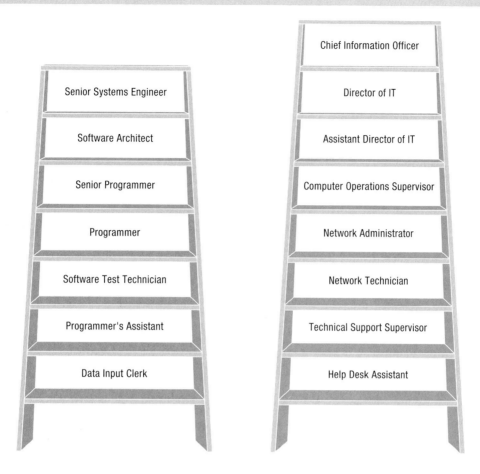

Thinking Critically Each job can help IT professionals move up in their careers. *What other IT jobs might help advance a career in information technology?*

- *Skills and Education* Computer engineers need substantial college-level education in engineering and excellent skills in programming, problem-solving, and logical analysis.

- **Computer Operator** Computer operators oversee the operation of mainframe computers and are often involved in networks of desktop computers.
  - *Skills and Education* Though computer operators must have excellent technical skills, they may not need more than an associate's degree from a technical college, plus substantial work experience and on-the-job training.

- **Computer Programmer** Computer programmers write, test, and maintain the instructions that tell a computer what to do. They often work with software engineers to design new software. Unlike software engineers, programmers usually write a custom program for a complex computer system.
  - *Skills and Education* Computer programmers need extensive experience with system design and maintenance, beginning with college-level education.

- **Computer Service Technician** Computer service technicians install, diagnose, and maintain computer hardware for everything from personal computers to entire mainframe-desktop systems.
  - *Skills and Education* A solid technical college education is a foundation for ongoing training in hardware developments.

- **Database Administrator** Database administrators manage the tremendous amounts of data that computers hold. They set up a database so that data can be not only stored but also retrieved when needed. They ensure that the data are not lost due to computer hackers, viruses, or technical malfunction.
  - *Skills and Education* Database administrators must understand, if not create, the software that handles the data under their management.

- **E-Commerce Specialist** E-commerce specialists create, manage, and maintain e-commerce Web sites. They work with a business to design a site that presents the company's products and allows customers to order them.
  - *Skills and Education* A college-level education may not be necessary, but it helps, especially for any services beyond the strictly technical. E-commerce specialists need to understand not only the technical aspects of creating a Web page, but also the potential responses of the users of that page.

- **Network Administrator** Network administrators install, maintain, and upgrade the hardware and software of networked computers and peripherals. Their duties include not only the connection of cables and adjustments of software, but also the instruction of people who use the network.
  - *Skills and Education* Network administrators must have excellent technical knowledge of computer hardware, operating systems, and electrical wiring.

- **Help Desk Technician/Technical Support Specialists** Technical support people help users of computer hardware and software when they have problems or questions.
  - *Skills and Education* Technical support is often an entry-level position for people who have a good technical background and are able to quickly learn the technologies of new products. They must be excellent problem-solvers and good communicators who can deal with angry or confused customers.

- **Technical Writer** Technical writers are often called upon to translate the technical language of computer engineers into a language that readers with no technical knowledge can understand.
  - *Skills and Education* Technical writers must have a strong command of language and writing, an ability to keep up with technical innovations, and solid organizational skills.

- **Web Designer** Web designers create the pages of the World Wide Web. They are an interesting blend of technician and artist, able to understand the logic of computers and the aesthetics of graphic design.
  - *Skills and Education* Web designers need technical and artistic knowledge. They must know the software used to create Web pages, and they often need to know programming languages.

Where Are the Jobs?

Most urban and industrial areas have jobs for IT professionals, though not all areas have jobs for all types of IT professionals. Large and medium-sized corporations and banks tend to need computer operators, network administrators, computer service

Pace Points

What Do You Know?

If you enjoy computers but are not sure if you know enough about them, talk to someone in the field and browse through a technical computer magazine. Do you know enough to start a career?

technicians, and database administrators. Most companies need a Web designer at some point, though they may not need one on staff.

A few areas of the United States have strong IT industries. The so-called Silicon Valley area of central California is the most famous, with hundreds of component and software development companies. New York City, the Boston area, and most other major cities also have strong IT industries.

International

IT professionals may find themselves with passports full of visas from foreign countries. Because so much software is developed in the United States, and because global companies depend on this software at offices in other countries, IT people are often sent around the world to install and maintain systems and to instruct people in the use of these systems. English is the universal language of information technology, so you won't necessarily need to speak a foreign language to do your job overseas. Still, it wouldn't hurt to learn a little of another language.

QUICK RECAP 1.2

INFORMATION TECHNOLOGY

- IT offers jobs wherever there are computers, and it is a rapidly growing field.
- The four IT career clusters include information support and services, programming and software development, network systems, and interactive media.
- Information support and services employs more people than any other IT pathway.
- Professionals in programming and software development design software and translate those designs into computer code.
- Network systems professionals support networks by installing network systems, fixing communication problems, and developing better ways for businesses to use networks.
- Professionals who work in this area of IT may be involved in Web page design, online payment systems, or the writing of technical assistance scripts.

CHECK YOURSELF

1. How could transferable skills help you shift your career path from Web page design to advertising?
2. Where in the United States are you most likely to find many IT positions?

Check your answers online at **www.mhhe.com/pace.** *Pace* ONLINE

BUSINESS VOCABULARY

virtual office   a portable office, consisting mostly of a laptop computer
network systems   links among computers and peripherals that enable several people to share software, files, computers, and peripherals at the same time
interactive media   electronic systems that allow users to input information and receive responses, as in computer games, chat rooms, and computer-based interactive training programs
e-commerce   business conducted over the Internet

Health Science

Health science—the medical field—offers some of the most gratifying professions. Professionals in health science relieve pain, prevent disease, and save lives. It is a profession of intelligent, caring people who are dedicated to helping others. The profession demands not only above-average education and training, but also above-average compassion for others. The jobs tend to pay above-average salaries, too.

It's About Helping People.   The health science career cluster offers a surprising variety of career pathways. These pathways lead into business administration, high technology, patient care, emergency rescue, scientific research, chemistry, biology, anatomy, and many other fields of study. Whatever direction you take, you will find yourself helping people.

Reading and Study Tip

Headings
Titles in text vary in size, boldness, and other details. How can you tell where the most important information is?

What Is Health Science?

Health science is the science of maintaining and improving human health. Job opportunities in health science range from health care—such as medical check-ups, surgery, vaccination, diagnosis and treatment of illness—to medical science involving scientific research into the prevention, treatment, and cure of health problems.

Occupations in health science are especially satisfying because they directly help improve lives. Professionals in the health sciences have helped to reduce the infant mortality rate—the percentage of infants who die in their first year of life—from 17 percent to less than 1 percent. The average life expectancy for Americans has risen to about 75 years, up 26 years from the early 1900s. Thanks to discoveries about nutrition and exercise, not to mention better medical treatments, people who live longer also live better, healthier, more active lives well into their later years.

The Health Science Workplace

Health science professionals work in a wide variety of places, including

- Hospitals
- Clinics and doctor's offices
- Laboratories
- Colleges and universities
- Nursing homes and long-term care facilities
- Assisted-living facilities
- Ambulances
- Industrial plants

Figure 1.4 *The Health Science Career Cluster*

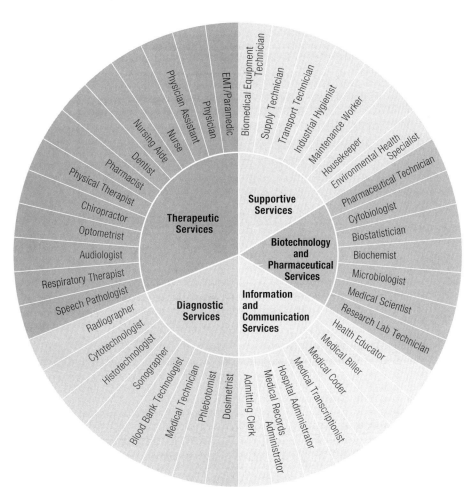

Thinking Critically Jobs in the health science career cluster involve planning, managing, and providing diagnostic, therapeutic, supportive, and information and research services. *How do your skills and interests fit with jobs in the health science cluster?*

The Health Science Career Cluster

The health science cluster can be divided into five career pathways (see Figure 1.4):

- Supportive services
- Information and communication services
- Diagnostic services
- Therapeutic services
- Biological and pharmaceutical services

Supportive Services

Health professionals who diagnose and treat health problems can't get much done without the vital services that support their efforts. Supportive services include administration, building and equipment maintenance, and environmental quality monitoring. Workers in supportive services face a special challenge: They work in places whose function is to care for the sick, yet they have to keep the environment exceptionally safe and hygienic. Their jobs extend across a wide range of education levels and salaries.

For example, industrial hygienists, also known as occupational safety and health specialists, minimize health hazards in workplaces. Environmental health specialists monitor air, water, and environmental quality in health care facilities. Biomedical equipment technicians and engineers maintain medical equipment, some of which is very technologically advanced. Building maintenance workers maintain health care facilities. Housekeepers clean health care workplaces, provide towels, change beds, and so on.

Preparation Housekeepers and building maintenance workers generally receive on-the-job training. Environmental and equipment technicians tend to have an associate or bachelor's degree. Industrial hygienists, environmental health specialists, and biomedical engineers need at least a bachelor's degree.

Information and Communication Services

Communication and the management of information are essential to safe, effective medical care. Medical and patient information must be carefully stored and easily retrieved. Communication among professionals and with the public must be effective.

Administrators handle much of the information involved in health science. Among administrators are admitting clerks, who receive patients into health care facilities; medical records administrators, who keep track of patient information; and hospital administrators, who take care of everything from staffing to accounting.

Educators are also an important part of health science. They teach professionals, from housekeepers to physicians, how to do their jobs. The also teach the public how to protect their health.

Preparation Professionals in information and communication services must be trained in the specifics of interpreting and managing medical information. Sometimes this involves training in the mechanics of specialized clerical work. High-level administrators may need master's degrees in business administration, information technology, library science, or public health. Educators may need bachelor's degrees and skills in writing and public speaking.

Diagnostic Services

diagnostic services the process of identifying disease and illness

Diagnostic services professionals identify disease and illness in patients. Imaging technicians take X-rays; perform MRI, PET, and CAT scans; and use ultrasound. Lab technicians use specialized equipment to assess the physical condition of a patient.

Preparation Professionals in diagnostic services need to be careful, precise, and observant workers who write accurate reports. Because their equipment is often highly technical, they need specialized training. They usually need at least an associate's degree in a health science area that would familiarize them with terminology and health care practices.

Therapeutic Services

therapeutic services treatment and therapy for diseases and disorders

Therapeutic services professionals provide treatment and therapy for diseases and disorders. Physical therapists help patients regain their mobility. Respiratory therapists help patients with breathing disorders. Home health aides provide assistance for patients at home. Dental hygienists provide preventive and therapeutic dental care. Pharmacists dispense prescription medicines. Emergency medical technicians

Square Peg

Your Challenge

As you interview for a new position, you realize that the actual job description does not fit your goals. What should you do?

The Possibilities

A. Ask about other available positions.

B. Pretend like you still want the job but don't accept any offers yet.

C. Ask questions to see if the job could still help you get where you want to be.

D. Explain to the interviewer that the job is not the one you wanted, thank him or her, then leave.

Your Solution

Choose the solution that you think will be the most effective and write a few sentences explaining your opinion on a separate piece of paper. Then check your answer with the answer at our Web site: **www.mhhe.com/pace.**

Pace
ONLINE

and paramedics provide emergency and ambulance services. Licensed practical nurses, registered nurses, and certified nurses aides provide various levels and types of patient care. Health practitioners are specially trained professionals such as dieticians, chiropractors, and midwives.

Preparation Training varies from the minimum of several college-level courses in a specialized area to a bachelor's or master's degree in a therapeutic specialty. Education must be ongoing to keep up with advances in medical practices and technology. Professionals also must have excellent skills in communication and observation as well as an ability to show compassion.

Biotechnology and Pharmaceutical Services

Professionals in biotechnology research and develop scientific techniques that improve health care. Pharmaceutical professionals research, develop, and dispense medicinal drugs. Both areas employ researchers who look for new ways to use technology to improve medical practices, equipment, and medicines. Developers in biotechnology and pharmacy use researchers' discoveries to produce new products.

Preparation Professionals have extensive education in the sciences, especially chemistry, biology, and statistics. Their mathematical and computer skills are exceptional, as are their ability to read and write technical material, observe the results of experiments, and communicate with nontechnical people.

❝ To be successful you have to be lucky or a little mad or very talented, or find yourself in a rapid growth field. ❞

Edward De Bono,
Physician, Educator

Jobs in Health Science

The health science career cluster offers opportunities in a wide variety of fields and at all levels of education and skill (Figure 1.5). Here are a few of the more common jobs, and the qualifications required to do them.

Figure 1.5 *Sample Career Ladders in Health Science*

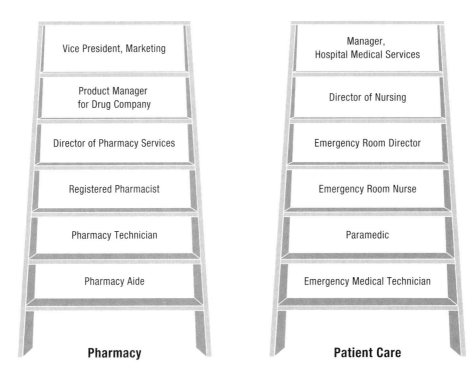

Pharmacy

Vice President, Marketing

Product Manager
for Drug Company

Director of Pharmacy Services

Registered Pharmacist

Pharmacy Technician

Pharmacy Aide

Patient Care

Manager,
Hospital Medical Services

Director of Nursing

Emergency Room Director

Emergency Room Nurse

Paramedic

Emergency Medical Technician

Thinking Critically Each job can help health science professionals move up in their careers. *What other jobs might help advance a career in health science?*

- **Home Health Aide** Home health aides assist the ill, the elderly, and people with disabilities by doing housework that their patients are unable to do. They also may perform basic medical assistance such as taking temperatures, changing bandages, and administering medications.
  - *Skills and Education* Home health aides don't need college-level education but may need training in basic health assistance.

- **Emergency Medical Technician/Paramedic** EMTs and paramedics usually provide emergency health care to patients while transporting them to a hospital. Paramedics give more advanced care, including emergency medications.
  - *Skills and Education* EMTs and paramedics need to take special courses and pass tests to become certified. Paramedics need college-level training.

- **Radiologic Technologist** Radiologic technologists use X-ray, MRI, and ultrasound equipment to produce images of the inside of a patient's body.
  - *Skills and Education* Radiologic technologists need specialized training in the equipment and procedures they use. A college-level background in science is helpful.

- **Registered Nurse** Registered nurses assist doctors in providing health care. They can administer medicine, advise patients, observe symptoms, record and interpret information, and educate the public authoritatively.
  - *Skills and Education* Nurses must complete intense college-level training, including education in biology and physiology.

Tips From a Mentor

Ten Fastest-Growing Occupations, Beginning with Those That Require the Least Training

- *Personal and home care assistants* help elderly or disabled adults with daily living activities. Need short-term, on-the-job training.

- *Social and human service assistants* assist professionals to provide client services for social and community services. Need on-the-job training.

- *Medical assistants* perform administrative and some clinical tasks under the direction of a doctor. Need on-the-job training.

- *Desktop publishers* format type and graphics for publication. Need post-secondary vocational certification.

- *Computer support specialists* provide technical assistance to computer system users. Need an associate's degree.

- *Computer software engineers* develop, create, and modify computer applications. Need a bachelor's degree.

- *Network and computer systems administrators and analysts* design, test, install, configure, and/or support a company's computer system. Need a bachelor's degree.

- *Database administrators* coordinate changes to computer databases. Need a bachelor's degree.

- *Computer systems analysts* analyze data processing systems. Need a bachelor's degree.

- *Physician's assistants* provide health care services. Need a bachelor's degree.

- **Pharmacist** Pharmacists specialize in the science of medicinal drugs. In some workplaces, pharmacists must be able to create prescription drugs from various ingredients.
  - *Skills and Education* Pharmacists need college-level education in chemistry, anatomy, physiology, and pharmacology.

- **Recreational Therapist** Recreational therapists help people with illnesses and disabilities stay physically and mentally fit. They not only organize exercise programs but also may counsel patients to help with emotional problems resulting from physical injury.
  - *Skills and Education* Recreational therapists need college-level education with a specialty in therapy.

- **Medical Transcriptionist** Medical transcriptionists listen to dictation recorded by doctors—usually information about patients—and transcribe that information to written form.
  - *Skills and Education* Medical transcriptionists need good typing skills and the ability to use word processing applications. They need to learn medical terminology.

Where Are the Jobs?

You will find jobs in health science where there are doctors, hospitals, nursing homes, clinics, assisted-living facilities, schools, or industrial plants. Hospitals offer the widest variety of opportunities. Schools need nurses and therapists who specialize in health and pediatric problems. Industrial plants need doctors and nurses specializing in occupational hazards and injuries. Any urban area will offer a wide variety of opportunities, especially in diagnostics and treatments involving high technology.

All populated regions of the United States need professionals in health science. If you want to work in a given geographic area, you should consider what kinds of health care facilities exist in that region. You can then assess potential career pathways.

International

Due to national regulations, international opportunities are limited. Most opportunities are in the marketing of pharmaceuticals.

QUICK RECAP 1.3

HEALTH SCIENCE

- Job opportunities in health science include both health care and medical research.
- There are health science opportunities in hospitals, clinics, nursing homes, schools, and industrial plants.
- Health science has five career clusters: supportive services, information and communication services, diagnostic services, therapeutic services, and biological and pharmaceutical services.
- The demand for health science professionals is expected to grow far faster than the national average for careers.
- Health science jobs are found in all populated areas, with the most variety in hospitals and urban areas.

CHECK YOURSELF

1. What do imaging technicians do?
2. Name ten health science jobs that put professionals in direct contact with patients.

Check your answers online at www.mhhe.com/pace.

BUSINESS VOCABULARY

diagnostic services   the process of identifying disease and illness
therapeutic services   treatment and therapy for diseases and disorders

Retail/Wholesale Sales and Service

Retail/wholesale sales and service is a vast and varied career cluster. Its workers include people in shipping, sales, advertising, product display, retail buying, management, and entrepreneurism. The cluster offers career ladders of many rungs. A store cashier can work his or her way up to become a store manager. A forklift operator can work his or her way up to become a manager of interstate shipping. The cluster almost seems designed for the purpose of offering opportunities to professionals who want to work hard to get ahead.

Satisfying Lives. Retail/wholesale sales and service is the very soul of the American economy. Ultimately, its purpose is to deliver to people the products and services they need to lead more satisfying lives. That process involves many activities, challenges, and opportunities for professionals who want to succeed in their careers.

What Is Retail/Wholesale Sales and Service?

Retail/wholesale sales and service is a crucial link in the process that delivers products to consumers. This link begins when the products leave the farm or manufacturing plant where they were produced. Products then follow a **distribution channel** that leads to customers.

The distribution channel may go first to **wholesalers:** businesses that buy large amounts of products. Wholesalers resell them to **retailers,** which are the businesses that sell products in small quantities to consumers, and often offer associated services such as installation and repair. Some retailers sell products in stores, while others sell only by mail, telephone, or the Internet. The retail industry is served by retailing services such as merchandising, product promotion, customer service, and advertising.

There are variations in these distribution channels. Some retailers buy directly from manufacturers. Some wholesalers sell directly to consumers. In **business-to-business** sales and service, the customer is a business that uses a product or service, or transforms a product into another product that is then sold.

The Retail/Wholesale Sales and Service Career Cluster

The wholesale/retail sales and service career cluster can be divided into four career pathways:

1. Merchandising and sales
2. Promotion and public relations
3. General distribution
4. Management/entrepreneurship

Reading and Study Tip

Taking Notes
When you take notes, don't copy information word for word. Use your own words and only write the most important facts.

distribution channel the route that products follow from manufacturing to customers

wholesaler a business that buys large volumes of products from manufacturers and sells them to retailers

retailer a business that sells products in small quantities to consumers, often with associated services such as installation and repair

business-to-business sales and service to other businesses that either use the product or service or transform the product into another product

---

Figure 1.6 *The Retail/Wholesale Sales & Service Career Cluster*

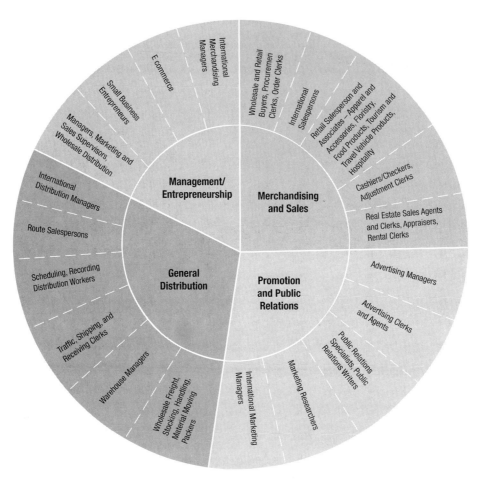

Thinking Critically Jobs in retail/wholesale sales and service involve planning, managing, and performing wholesaling and retailing services and related marketing and distribution support services, including merchandising/product management and promotion. *How do your skills and interests fit with jobs in the sales and service career cluster?*

Merchandising and Sales

merchandising the planning, developing, and presenting of a company's product lines

Merchandising is the planning, developing, and presenting of a company's product lines. Sales, of course, is the process of helping customers understand how a product can satisfy their needs.

Careers in merchandising and sales relate to promoting, buying, and presenting goods to the public and to businesses. Retail buyers plan and purchase products that will be sold by stores and other retailers. Sales representatives work directly with customers, be they consumers or businesses, to show them how products can satisfy their needs. Cashiers and checkers receive money from retail customers.

Real estate agents help property buyers buy houses and business locations. Display coordinators prepare store product displays to attract customers. Product managers, usually employed by manufacturers, oversee all the details of getting a particular line of products from the manufacturer to the retailer.

Social Drinks

Your Challenge

A person who is a very important customer invites you for a drink in the hotel bar. You soon perceive that he's a big drinker who would like you to keep up with him. What would be a good sequence of moves for you? What would you definitely avoid?

The Possibilities

A. Match him drink for drink.

B. Tell him he's drinking too much.

C. Drink all you want and leave the tab for him to pay.

D. Have one drink, agree to meet in the future, pay the tab, shake his hand, say thank you, and leave.

Your Solution

Choose the solution that you think will be the most effective and write a few sentences explaining your opinion on a separate piece of paper. Then check your answer with the answer on our Web site: **www.mhhe.com/pace.**

Preparation   The sales and merchandising career pathway has many entry-level jobs, such as cashier and sales assistant, that require no previous training. Other positions, such as product manager, require a bachelor's degree. Merchandising professionals generally need training and experience in a specific product area.

Promotion and Public Relations

Promotion and public relations professionals have the responsibility of ensuring that products have buyers. They do this through advertising and other promotional activities.

Advertising managers create and oversee advertising campaigns. Marketing managers create plans to showcase a company's products and services. Public relations account executives help a client manufacturer or business improve its public image through special events, newspaper and magazine articles, and television coverage. Copywriters write advertisements and press releases that announce product and company news to the media.

Preparation   Even entry-level jobs in promotion and public relations require a bachelor's degree, preferably with a major in a related area such as communication, business, or marketing. Management-level jobs require years of experience.

General Distribution

General distribution is the process of shipping the right goods to the right place at the right time. **Logistics** is the management of all the details of general distribution. Warehouse managers ensure that incoming products are properly stored and outgoing products get onto the right trucks. Freight and stock handlers do the physical moving of products in the warehouse. International distribution managers organize the transfer of goods across international borders.

logistics the management of all the details of general distribution

Preparation   Freight and stock handlers are usually trained on the job. Managers usually have a bachelor's degree in business or management and a good sense of working within a system.

Management/Entrepreneurship

Management and entrepreneur professionals are the managers who lead a business and make sure it works. In large retail stores, individual managers oversee marketing, merchandising, buying, and general types of products such as clothing, jewelry, and tools. **Entrepreneurs** are the professionals who assume the risks of new business and lead efforts to improve and expand existing business.

entrepreneurs professionals who assume the risks of new business and lead efforts to improve and expand existing business

Preparation   Managers need a bachelor's or master's degree in an area of business. Managers organize people and projects and oversee every activity in their departments. Entrepreneurs need to be creative and dynamic in developing business.

Jobs in Wholesale/Retail Sales and Service

Career pathways in wholesale and retail offer complete career ladders from entry-level positions through top management (Figure 1.7). The most successful career ladders will launch the professional into the exciting and challenging position of entrepreneur. Here is a sampling of the scores of job titles found in retail and wholesale.

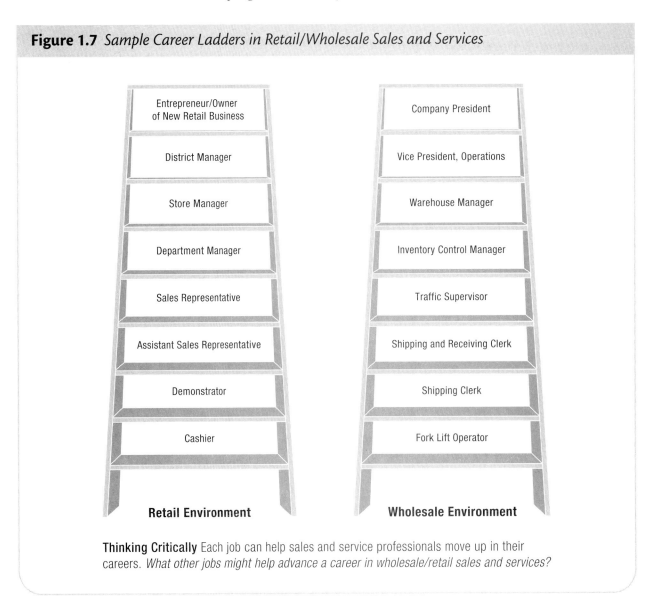

Figure 1.7 *Sample Career Ladders in Retail/Wholesale Sales and Services*

Retail Environment
- Entrepreneur/Owner of New Retail Business
- District Manager
- Store Manager
- Department Manager
- Sales Representative
- Assistant Sales Representative
- Demonstrator
- Cashier

Wholesale Environment
- Company President
- Vice President, Operations
- Warehouse Manager
- Inventory Control Manager
- Traffic Supervisor
- Shipping and Receiving Clerk
- Shipping Clerk
- Fork Lift Operator

Thinking Critically Each job can help sales and service professionals move up in their careers. *What other jobs might help advance a career in wholesale/retail sales and services?*

Entry-Level Positions

Entry-level positions require no more than high school education. Employers usually provide on-the-job training.

- *Adjustment clerks* help customers who have experienced problems with the products they bought. The adjustment clerk decides whether the customer should receive money back, a new product, or another form of compensation.
- *Cashiers* operate cash registers as they check purchases, often by scanning their bar code.
- *Customer service representatives* help customers with questions and problems.
- *Demonstrators* show potential customers how to use products or offer samples.
- *Inventory clerks* keep track of quantities of products in storage.
- *Shipping and receiving clerks* take care of the paperwork involved in sending or receiving shipments.
- *Telemarketers* call potential customers by phone to offer products.

Mid-Level Positions

Mid-level positions demand experience that proves a certain level of responsibility and intelligence. Some jobs require college education and/or in-house training.

- *Account executives* oversee a professional-level service, such as advertising or public relations, for a client company.
- *Administrative assistants* help managers and executives do their jobs by taking care of nondecisional activities.
- *Customer service managers* oversee customer service representatives.
- *Department managers* oversee retail departments such as jewelry, shoes, appliances, and so on.
- *Marketing researchers* plan and execute strategies for advertising the right product in the right market.
- *Real estate agents* represent the sellers of buildings and property by helping buyers find the real estate they need.
- *Traffic managers* coordinate the movement of products, projects, or shipments.

Management Level Positions

Management positions require not only a college degree but also some years of solid experience in the field.

- *Account supervisors* manage account executives and various aspects of services for a client company.
- *Buyers* (retail or wholesale) assess products and decide which to buy for subsequent resale.
- *District managers* oversee sales representatives in an area determined by the company or in several chain stores in an area.
- *Entrepreneurs* start new businesses or expand and improve existing businesses.
- *Marketing managers* oversee advertising, public relations, merchandising, promotions, packaging, and other aspects of marketing.
- *Store designers* plan the layout of stores to maximize product visibility, control the movement of customers, ensure safety, and make the movement of products easier.

New Attitudes / New Opportunities

Meet Roxi Maina. Roxi is originally from Cartagena, Colombia, but moved with her family to the United States when she was ten. She is a wife and mother of three and currently works as an administrator with Adecco Staffing in Pembroke Pines, Florida. Roxi started out as a crossing guard and worked her way up. She has taken several different job skill courses and worked in different industries and positions throughout her professional life. Here's what she has to say about . . .

How She Developed a Career   "My home life was always my priority, because I had small kids. Then I saw an ad at my son's middle school about being a crossing guard, only working two hours a day and having holidays off. That's how I became involved with Adecco. I was very happy being a crossing guard. Then I got a call from the office with some questions for me. I said, 'I can help you with that. If you ever need a supervisor, let me know.' I did not know at the time that they did need a supervisor! I got the position and worked up from there. I didn't plan my career, but whatever job I had, I always had a good work ethic: I worked hard and tried to go the extra mile. You know, maximizing on any opportunity that's there and having a good attitude, so people see that I am somebody that cares and wants to do a good job."

On How "Temping" Can Be a Good Way to See Different Industries and Narrow Down What You Want to Do   "Working here at the office, I see how a lot of different people are using temp agencies for the opportunity to try different jobs and fields. It is a great opportunity for someone switching careers or who is not sure what he or she wants to do."

On What to Look for In a Job   "You always want to be in a position where you are using your skills and you are happy. You should ask yourself, 'Is this the kind of environment I want to be in?' Some people are really not office people—some people like being outside or on the road. The last thing anyone wants is to be in a job where he or she is not using his or her gifts and talents. If there is something that you know you want, get whatever education you need to get to it."

On Getting an Education and What You Can Do to Learn the Skills You Need   "I don't draw a line where if you get an education you're in and if you don't get an education you are going to be pumping gas for the rest of your life. I've seen people who have an education that are worthless when they get into the workforce and I also have seen people who were unable to get an education but who have what it takes. Getting a college education was just never an option for me when I was younger. I did take advantage of courses that work paid for and did some on my own. If you apply yourself, no matter where you are, you will succeed."

Where Are the Jobs?

Jobs in retail/wholesale sales and service are all over the map and all over the business world. Towns of all sizes have retail stores. Medium-sized towns typically have wholesalers, distribution centers, or warehouses, usually located near interstate highways or airports. Regions of the country with thriving economies will have the most jobs in this cluster, especially in retail. Wholesale and distribution are often found in less populated regions.

International

Wholesale/retail business is global, with channels of distribution reaching around the world. Product managers may go to manufacturing plants in Asia and South America. Advertising and marketing managers often have to coordinate projects with people from other countries. Top-level managers sometimes reside in foreign countries long enough to organize retail stores and distribution centers. Wholesale buyers and buyers from large stores travel the world in search of products. International logistics professionals are in constant contact with overseas shippers.

English is the language of international business, so you won't necessarily need to know a foreign language to do your job overseas. Still, you will see that people can usually read written English a lot more easily than they can understand spoken English.

Business-to-Business

A great deal of marketing and sales is directed at businesses. Business-to-business sales are generally much larger than sales to individual consumers, and sales presentations may take weeks of planning. Sales are not made in retail stores, but rather by sales representatives who participate in trade shows and contact customer companies.

QUICK RECAP 1.4

RETAIL/WHOLESALE SALES AND SERVICE

- The wholesale/retail sales and service career cluster starts where products leave manufacturing plants and ends where products are sold to customers.
- Wholesalers buy products in large volumes and sell them to retailers who sell them to individual consumers.
- The four career pathways in this cluster are (1) merchandising and sales, (2) promotion and public relations, (3) general distribution, and (4) management/entrepreneurship.
- Merchandising and sales present products to the customer, with jobs ranging from retail buyer to sales representative to cashier.
- Promotion and public relations includes advertising.
- General distribution is the process of shipping goods to the right place at the right time.
- Managers and entrepreneurs are the decision makers who ensure that a business works.
- Wholesale/retail business is global, with channels of distribution reaching around the world.

CHECK YOURSELF

1. What is the difference between wholesale, retail, and business-to-business?
2. In which career pathway would logistics professionals work?

Check your answers online at **www.mhhe.com/pace.**

BUSINESS VOCABULARY

distribution channel   the route that products follow from manufacturing to customers
wholesaler   a business that buys large volumes of products from manufacturers and sells them to retailers
retailer   a business that sells products in small quantities to consumers, often with associated services such as installation and repair
business-to-business   sales and service to other businesses that either use the product or service or transform the product into another product
merchandising   the planning, developing, and presenting of a company's product lines
logistics   the management of all the details of general distribution
entrepreneurs   professionals who assume the risks of new business and lead efforts to improve and expand existing business

Communication and Media

Communication is the fascinating field in which information meets technology to help people share ideas. Without communication professionals, business would simply stop, and society would return to the dark ages. Today, the field of communication and media industries brings us books, magazines, newspapers, telephone service, pagers, cable television, photography, choreography, music, desktop publishing, film, and many other ways of moving information and ideas.

Moving ideas and information. Communication and media is a career cluster that extends from the beauty of the arts to the power of media and technology. The career pathways through this cluster go in many directions. Which is right for you? **Communication** is the act of moving ideas and information. **Communication media** are the ways that ideas and information are moved, including print, motion pictures, telephones, television, speech, computers, the Internet, and arts such as dance, music, photography, sculpting, and painting. When we speak of *the media,* we are often referring to the industries that bring us news, entertainment, information, and art.

Reading and Study Tip

Margin Features
Look at the text in the margins. What kind of information does It give? Why is it in the margin instead of in a paragraph on the page?

communication the act of moving ideas and information

communication media the ways that ideas and information are moved or carried

The Communication Workplace

Communication and media workplaces are as varied as the industries that make up this career cluster. They include

- Television studios
- Print shops
- Business offices
- Motion picture sets
- Newspaper and magazine offices
- Theaters
- Home offices

Working conditions can vary greatly. Most involve high-technology tools such as computers, telephone systems, satellite communication equipment, and cameras. Some professionals may spend all day at a desk, doing their work on a computer screen. Some may be outdoors for many hours at a time. Newspaper offices may be busy and stressful. Television studios may demand intense focus as other people work nearby. Many independent professionals, such as writers and graphic artists, do freelance work from home offices.

Some workplaces can be very exciting. Journalists travel to government offices, disaster sights, and crime scenes. Documentary film crews visit mountaintops, rainforests, deserts, and foreign countries. Actors and musicians play on stages all over the world.

Figure 1.8 *The Arts, Audio/Video Technology, and Communications Career Cluster*

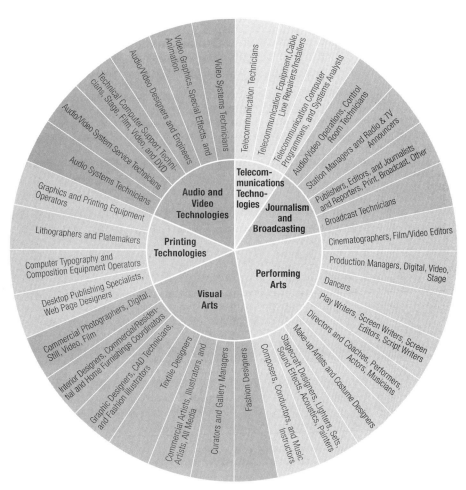

Thinking Critically Jobs in the communication and media career cluster involve designing, producing, exhibiting, performing, writing, publishing, journalism, and entertainment. *How do your skills and interests fit with jobs in the communication and media career cluster?*

The Communication and Media Career Cluster

The communication and media cluster can be divided into six main segments:

- Telecommunication technologies
- Audio and video technologies
- Journalism, publishing, and broadcast
- Printing technologies
- Visual arts
- Performing arts

Telecommunication Technologies

Telecommunication technologies include radio, telephone, and the Internet. While the content of these media are produced in other segments such as journalism and entertainment, the technological segment includes the equipment and links that make communication possible. This equipment includes telephones, wires, cables, satellites, fax machines, computers, radios, and pagers.

Preparation Telecommunication professionals tend to be highly trained in specific technologies. They usually have a college degree of at least an associate level, with certification in their area of expertise, plus even more specialized training provided by their employers. Training must be constantly renewed to keep up with technology.

Audio and Video Technologies

Professionals in audio/video technology are engineers and technicians who design, install, maintain, and repair audio and video equipment. Some work for manufacturers, others for retail stores, and others for business-to-business companies. Some work for television and radio studios. Some work for the corporations and schools that use this equipment.

Preparation Technicians usually have at least an associate's degree. Engineers generally need at least a bachelor's degree in engineering. On-the-job training with specific equipment is usually necessary. Sometimes training is provided by the manufacturers of equipment.

Journalism, Publishing, and Broadcasting

The majority of journalists work for newspapers ranging from the big daily papers to small local weeklies. About a third of journalists work in radio and television, most of them behind the scenes to find and write the news that the anchors read to the public. This segment also includes everyone involved in producing programs, writing scripts, managing stations, and operating broadcast equipment.

The publishing industry offers opportunities to editors, graphic designers, writers, and advertisers.

Preparation Journalists and editors are expected to have at least a bachelor's degree, usually in journalism, English, writing, or communication. They need to have good writing skills and an ability to work well under pressure. People in broadcast production usually have a degree in communication or video production, plus training in the use of specific equipment. They need to be able to work in a stressful workplace where every task must be executed perfectly, and at exactly the right time.

Printing Technologies

Printing technology is the technology used to print newspapers, magazines, brochures, catalogs, and other documents. The professionals who work in this industry include Web site designers and graphic designers.

Preparation Graphic artists need an associate or bachelor's degree in design, art, or Web site development. Professionals in the printing industry have either an associate's degree in printing technology or substantial on-the-job training.

Visual Arts

Professionals in the visual arts include commercial artists, fine artists, photographers, videographers, fashion designers, art instructors, and museum curators.

Over half of them are self-employed, most of them working with desktop publishing systems (computer applications for working with graphics) at home offices. They work for advertising agencies, book publishers, the motion picture and television industries, and companies that design anything from Web sites to fabrics.

Preparation   Visual artists need artistic talent, which is usually developed in college-level courses. They often need good computer graphic skills. Professional experience not only improves their skills but gives them a **portfolio**—a collection of their best work—to impress potential future employers.

portfolio a collection of an artist's best work

Performing Arts

The performing arts include such talents as acting, singing, dancing, composing, and conducting as well as the behind-the-scenes jobs that make performances possible. These supporting jobs include writing, directing, cinematography, film editing, set design, lighting, production management, and make-up art. The talent side of the industry is renowned for its competition. Most artists hold other jobs outside of the field.

Preparation   Talent, of course, is essential to success in the performing arts. Backstage workers must be creative and driven to succeed. A degree from a performing arts school can be helpful. In most technical fields, such as film and video production, a college degree is important, as is practical experience.

❝ I don't care if his skills are weak and he's got no experience. Look at that enthusiasm and energy level. He's going to be terrific. ❞

Edgar Trenner,
Director, Camp Arcady

Jobs in Communication and Media

Communication and media have opportunities for those who like to work with ideas, information, words, and images and those who like technical jobs involving cables and equipment (Figure 1.9). Here are just a few of the wide variety of jobs in this career cluster:

- **Broadcast Technician** Broadcast technicians operate and maintain the electronic equipment used to transmit radio and television programs. Specialists in this area include audio control technicians, video control technicians, recording engineers, and field technicians who work with portable broadcast equipment.
  - *Skills and Education* Technicians need college-level training in basic electronics and specialized training in the equipment they use. They may need certification or a license.
- **Computer Animator** Computer animators use computers and special software to create moving cartoon images for movies, advertisements, video games, and other venues.
  - *Skills and Education* Computer animation demands technical know-how and an artistic eye for the colors, angles, and lighting that simulate real movement. Though college-level courses may help develop skills, employers tend to make decisions based on examples of previous work.
- **Cable Television Technician** Cable television technicians install and repair equipment for cable broadcasters and individual users.
  - *Skills and Education* Cable television technicians need basic electronics classes and on-the-job training.
- **Commercial Artist** Commercial artists, also known as graphic artists, design and produce artwork for advertisements, magazine and book publishing, Web sites, video production, and other venues that use images for business purposes.
  - *Skills and Education* Commercial artists need artistic ability and a working knowledge of the computer software used in graphic art. Employers may prefer someone with an associate's degree.

Figure 1.9 *Sample Career Ladders in Journalism and Television Media*

Journalism

- Editor-in-Chief
- Managing Editor
- News Editor
- Assistant News Editor
- Reporter
- Copy Editor

Television

- Director of Programming
- Studio Manager
- Program Director
- Video Technician
- Camera Operator

Thinking Critically Each job can help communication and media professionals move up in their careers. *What other jobs might help advance a career in communication or media?*

wire services news organizations that sell articles and photos to the press

- **Journalist** Journalists gather news and information for newspapers, magazines, broadcasters, and **wire services,** which are news organizations that sell articles and photos to the press. Editors give journalists assignments, though some freelance journalists sell articles to an editor.
  - *Skills and Education* Employers usually look for a bachelor's degree in journalism, English, history, writing, or communication. Specialized trade magazines may prefer some credits in a related field.
- **Telecommunications Technician** Telecommunications technicians install, test, and maintain telephone, radio, fiber optic, and satellite transmission equipment and systems. Their work can include everything from installing cables to programming computers.
  - *Skills and Education* Telecommunications technicians need a basic understanding of electronics, usually gained through community college courses.

Where Are the Jobs?

Jobs in communication and media tend to be in urban and commercial areas. Journalists can find jobs at local newspapers, but the better-paying jobs at larger papers, magazines, and broadcasters are found in larger cities. Large and medium-sized companies are the main employers of commercial artists. Many writers, editors, and artists are able to work from home as freelancers, often using the Internet to send their work to distant clients.

International

Sometimes companies and publications send communications personnel on foreign assignments. Technicians in fields of high technology are often needed for new installations or to instruct local people on the use of equipment. Wire services and the major newspapers and magazines have correspondents in foreign capitals. Freelance writers, photographers, and video news teams can contribute material from other countries. Technical writers and translators may be sent to business sites in major cities and industrial sites in remote areas. Other communications professionals may be sent to conferences and trade shows in major cities in Europe and Asia.

Business-to-Business

Most of the communication and media industry is in business-to-business service. Most technicians work for one company that installs or maintains equipment at another company. Many video producers do jobs only for corporations. Firms specializing in graphic arts and design serve corporate clients. Many freelancers practice their art while providing corporate clients with valued services.

QUICK RECAP 1.5

COMMUNICATION AND MEDIA

- Communication is the act of moving ideas and information, and communication media are the means of communication, such as print, television, and the Internet.
- The communication and media industry covers telecommunication; audio and visual technologies; journalism, publishing, and broadcasting; printing technologies; visual arts; and performance arts.
- Most jobs in communication and media demand a college degree; many hiring decisions are based on experience and portfolios.
- Over half of the professionals in visual arts are self-employed and many work from home offices.
- There are international opportunities for technicians in high technology and for journalists and photographers who work for major publications.

CHECK YOURSELF

1. Which communication and media career pathways offer opportunities for freelancers?
2. Which career pathways require professionals to keep up with technology?

Check your answers online at **www.mhhe.com/pace.** *Pace* ONLINE

BUSINESS VOCABULARY

communication   the act of moving ideas and information
communication media   the ways that ideas and information are moved or carried
portfolio   a collection of an artist's best work
wire services   news organizations that sell articles and photos to the press

Finance and Accounting

For those who are unfamiliar with the business world, the word *finance* can conjure images of stockbrokers wildly shouting buy and sell orders on Wall Street, or of accountants cranking adding machines all day long. A more realistic picture, however, would show top-level management accountants working with CEOs to plan a new business, or a banker meeting with a young couple to help them buy their first home, or investment brokers studying a company to determine whether its stock will rise in value.

The Money Business. The movement of money in global, national, and local economies is like the movement of blood through the arteries and veins of a body. Like blood, money has to flow to the right places in the right amounts at the right time to keep a nation's economy healthy. Professionals in the business of finance and accounting make sure that happens.

Reading and Study Tip

Diagrams
Sometimes information is easier to understand when presented in a diagram rather than in paragraph form. Find a paragraph that can be translated into a diagram in order to make the facts more clear.

finance the business of acquiring, investing, and managing money

accounting the business of watching, measuring, and recording the movement of money and other assets

asset Something with value

What Is Finance and Accounting?

Finance is the business of acquiring, investing, and managing money. **Accounting** is the business of watching, measuring, and recording the movement of money and other things with value, known as **assets.** There is no definite line distinguishing finance from accounting. The two overlap in many ways.

Money and other assets include loans, mortgages, stocks, bonds, interest rates, real estate, factory equipment, foreign currencies, and the right to buy corn at a certain price. Money and assets take so many forms that professionals can hardly keep up with their constant evolution.

Finance and Accounting Workplaces

Financial professionals work in

- Banks, including commercial, investment, and savings banks;
- Brokerages that help individuals, companies, and governments make investments;
- Insurance companies that help individuals and organizations reduce their risk of financial loss;
- Corporations that need their financial assets managed and invested efficiently;
- Public accounting firms that audit company financial records;
- Not-for-profit organizations; and
- Government offices (federal, state, and municipal).

The Finance and Accounting Career Pathways

The finance and accounting career cluster (Figure 1.10) can be divided into four career pathways:

Figure 1.10 *The Business and Administration Career Cluster*

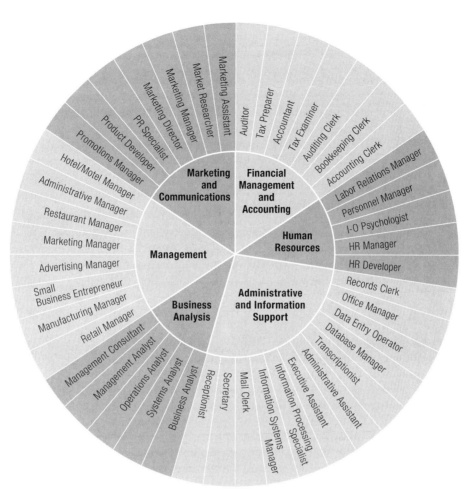

Thinking Critically Financial professionals provide services for financial and investment planning, banking, insurance, and business financial management and auditing. *How do your skills and interests fit with jobs in the finance and accounting career cluster?*

- Banking and related services
- Insurance services
- Financial and investment planning
- Business financial management

Banking and Related Services

Banking and related services include many positions in commercial, savings, and investment banks.

- *Bank tellers* help customers make deposits and withdrawals, make payments, and buy travelers' checks and money orders. New account clerks help customers open and close checking and savings accounts.

- *Loan and credit clerks* process the paperwork of loans and lines of credit.
- *Loan officers* evaluate loan applications to verify whether applicants will probably be able to repay the loans.
- *Collection officers* take the actions necessary to collect unpaid loans.
- *Money desk clerks* handle wire transfers of money.
- *Branch managers* make sure bank offices are following procedures properly.

Preparation   Very careful attention to detail and working within strict guidelines are the fundamental skills of everyone in banking. An associate's degree in a related area will make it easier to land an entry-level position. Subsequent in-house training will allow advancement to other positions. A bachelor's degree is necessary for office positions. Controllers, vice presidents, and financial analysts need experience and a master's degree.

Insurance Services

Professionals in the insurance industry help individuals, companies, governments, and other organizations minimize financial risk. Some work directly with customers. Others work within the insurance company headquarters to assess risk and manage the tremendous amounts of money involved.

- *Insurance agents* and brokers sell insurance policies through local offices that represent the insurance company.
- *Underwriters* determine how much coverage is needed and what it will cost.
- *Appraisers* estimate the value of items that are to be insured.
- *Adjusters* determine whether claims are covered by customers' policies.
- *Actuaries* analyze statistics to calculate the extent of risk and the consequent cost of insurance.

Preparation   Insurance professionals must have excellent analytical and problem-solving skills. Adjusters, agents, underwriters, and actuaries need a college degree. Brokers and agents must have licenses issued in their state.

Financial and Investment Planning

Financial and investment planning professionals include financial advisors, stockbrokers, and real estate asset managers. Their job is to help people keep their money safe and growing and their real estate productive. Typical investments are in **stock,** which are partial ownerships of companies; **bonds,** which are corporate and government written promises to repay specific amounts of money in the future; and **commodities,** which are products regarded as basic goods, such as cotton, oil, coffee, and lumber.

- *Financial advisors* counsel clients on investments, retirement planning, insurance planning, tax strategies, and similar money matters.
- *Stockbrokers* buy and sell securities (stocks and bonds) and commodities for their clients.
- *Real estate asset managers* help real estate owners keep their properties productive.
- *Tax preparers* help individuals file tax returns.

Preparation   Financial planning and investment requires considerable education—a bachelor's degree at least, a master's degree ideally. In many areas, related trade associations grant certification. Professionals in this area need strong skills in math and analysis and in working with clientele who understand little about financial planning.

Dr. Joe Pace
RISK

"You cannot discover new oceans unless you have the courage to lose sight of the shore."

stock an investment that gives partial ownership of a company

bond a corporate or government written promise to repay a specific amount in the future

commodities products regarded as basic goods, such as cotton, oil, coffee, and lumber

Business Financial Management

Business financial management covers two general areas: corporate and auditing. Auditing is a check of a company's financial records to make sure they are accurate and fairly represented. Audits are required of all public companies, that is, companies owned by stockholders. Other companies are often audited to provide information to the institutions that lend them money.

On the corporate side, financial managers and management accountants direct a company's investments so that money, equipment, and personnel are kept productive. They also produce the company's financial reports. At the upper level of their profession, they are part of a corporation's top management. Cost accountants calculate the cost of manufacturing, marketing, and delivering products. Internal auditors verify that financial matters are in proper order, watch for fraud, and report on risks to the business. Controllers and chief financial officers oversee the preparation of financial documents that are issued to both investors and the Securities and Exchange Commission. Corporate accountants keep track of financial transactions and file tax returns. Bookkeepers record financial transactions.

Public accountants, also known as auditors or certified public accountants (CPAs), work for independent audit firms that check the financial records of companies so that investors and creditors know what they are getting into. They often advise corporate management on financial matters.

Preparation   Most levels of business financial management require a bachelor's degree at the very least, though bookkeepers can start with an associate's degree. To perform audits, professionals must become CPAs by earning a four-year degree and then completing an additional year of special professional education. They also must pass an examination. Certifications in other areas, such as management accounting and internal auditing, will help career advancement. All financial and accounting professionals need to keep up with the latest financial software.

Jobs in Finance and Accounting

Jobs in finance and accounting range from entry-level positions (Figure 1.11), which often involve little more than recording information, to top management, where decisions are made. Here are just a few:

- **Budget Analyst** Budget analysts develop budgets for companies, departments, projects, new product development, and so forth. They determine the most efficient way to allocate resources.
    - *Skills and Education* Budget analysts usually have a bachelor's degree in a related field, such as accounting, mathematics, or economics.
- **Stockbroker** Stockbrokers are licensed to buy and sell stock, bonds, and commodities for their clients. Some stockbrokers also sell other financial products, such as insurance policies and annuities.
    - *Skills and Education* Stockbrokers must be able to understand financial reports and explain opportunities to clients. A bachelor's degree and business experience are needed.
- **Financial Planner** Financial planners help clients establish and meet financial goals by investing money wisely. They help clients put together a portfolio (a balanced group of various investments), which may include stocks and bonds, insurance policies, real estate, and money market accounts.
    - *Skills and Education* Financial planners must be educated in investment strategies, tax laws, insurance, and estate planning. Most have a bachelor's degree in a financial major. Certification in financial planning helps but is not required.

Figure 1.11 *Sample Career Ladders in Finance and Accounting*

Finance ladder (bottom to top):
- Brokerage Clerk
- Stockbroker
- Stock Analyst
- Portfolio Manager
- Vice President, Investment Services

Finance

Accounting ladder (bottom to top):
- Teller
- Head Teller
- Customer Service Representative
- New Account Clerk
- Mortgage Loan Officer
- Branch Manager
- Bank Manager

Accounting

Thinking Critically Each job can help finance and accounting professionals move up in their careers. *What other jobs might help advance a career in finance or accounting?*

- **Insurance Underwriter** Underwriters help insurance companies evaluate risk to determine how much insurance coverage is needed and how much it should cost.
  - *Skills and Education* Underwriters need excellent math and computer skills. A bachelor's degree is recommended, as is the ability to research and analyze information.

- **Loan Officer** Loan officers help bank clients apply for loans and help banks decide which loans to make. Commercial loan officers work with businesses that need to buy equipment or make other investments. Consumer loan officers help individuals borrow money. Mortgage loan officers work with mortgages.
  - *Skills and Education* Loan officers must be skilled in math and information analysis.

Where Are the Jobs?

There are accounting and finance opportunities wherever there are banks and corporations. Insurance professionals are needed wherever people own houses and cars and wherever businesses operate. The greatest opportunities in banking are in the country's major financial centers: New York; Boston; Washington, D.C.; Chicago; Los Angeles; and San Francisco. Investment brokerages are concentrated in New York, Boston, and Chicago. Corporations hire most of their corporate accountants at their headquarters, which tend to be found in the East between Boston and Washington, D.C., and in Chicago, Dallas, Los Angeles, San Francisco, Seattle, Atlanta, and other major cities. All large and medium-sized cities have offices of the international accounting firms, and small cities usually have a few smaller CPA practices.

International

International corporations, banks, and insurance companies very often send financial professionals overseas to coordinate foreign offices. Public and tax accountants tend to stay within the country where they know the laws and regulations. A new system of international accounting standards may soon make it easier to apply accounting rules in different countries. Cost accountants and internal auditors often go to foreign offices of U.S. corporations on temporary and long-term assignments. English is the language of international business, so the management-level people you deal with will probably speak it fluently.

Business-to-Business

Commercial and investment banks tend to serve other businesses. Public accounting firms are, by definition, business-to-business service providers. The business-to-business segment of the insurance industry is complex and high powered, with any given account involving a variety of insurance professionals. Business-to-business financial professionals must have top-notch education and skills to deliver excellent service to other professionals, who expect wise advice and perfectly executed assignments.

QUICK RECAP 1.6

FINANCE AND ACCOUNTING

- Financial professionals manage money; accounting professionals measure and record the movement of money.
- Financial and accounting professionals find jobs in banking, insurance, and financial planning and investment, as well as in business financial management and auditing.
- Banks offer many entry-level opportunities for clerks and tellers, and in-house training can lead to higher positions.
- Insurance professionals help companies and individuals minimize their risk of financial loss.
- Financial and investment planning professionals help their clients keep their money and real estate productive.
- Business financial management includes corporate (or management) accountants and public auditors.
- Generally, the job outlook for finance and accounting professionals is very good, especially for those with higher education and up-to-date financial technology skills.

CHECK YOURSELF

1. What is the difference between finance and accounting?
2. Why is banking a good place to start a career for someone with an associate's degree?

Check your answers online at **www.mhhe.com/pace.**

BUSINESS VOCABULARY

finance the business of acquiring, investing, and managing money

accounting the business of watching, measuring, and recording the movement of money and other assets

asset something with value

stock an investment that gives partial ownership of a company

bond a corporate or government written promise to repay a specific amount in the future

commodities products regarded as basic goods, such as cotton, oil, coffee, and lumber

Chapter Summary

1.1 Career Directions

Objective: *Look at the many directions a career can take and the importance of developing transferable skills during your professional growth.*

In this section, you learned that transferable skills, such as the ability to analyze information, write clearly, and work well with others, will help you shift your career from one pathway to another. You learned the importance of continuing your education to keep up with technology and changes in your industry. You saw an overview of five career clusters.

1.2 Information Technology

Objective: *Examine some of the jobs in the country's fastest-growing industry and understand the importance of continuously upgrading your skills to keep up with technology.*

Information technology offers a wide variety of professions, from the designing of computer chips to the building of computers to the development of software applications. The jobs are not only at computer and software companies, but at banks, corporations, government offices, schools—just about everywhere you find computers.

1.3. Health Science

Objective: *Learn about the potential rewards of a job in the health sciences.*

Health science offers career pathways that go in various directions, all of them interesting and satisfying. All of them help people lead better and longer lives. Career pathways can go into the services that support doctors and other medical workers or the therapeutic services that deal directly with patients, diagnostics, and research services.

1.4 Retail/Wholesale Sales and Service

Objective: *Recognize the jobs involved in bringing products from the manufacturing plant to the hands of the final customer.*

Jobs in retail/wholesale sales and service include product management, shipping, marketing, advertising, public relations, packaging, design, merchandising, sales, and every other activity that takes place between the manufacturing plant and the exchange of product for payment. This career cluster begins with simple jobs in retail stores and can reach to the development of a new business.

1.5 Communication and Media

Objective: *Examine a career cluster that includes both the technicians that make modern communication and media work and the creative people who provide information and entertainment to the public.*

Professionals in communication and media bring us movies, television programs, books, magazines, newspapers, Web sites, arts, and other forms of information and entertainment. The industry needs technical people to install, maintain, and work with communication technology such as telephone systems, broadcast equipment, film production, and printing operations. It also needs writers, illustrators, designers, artists, and entertainers.

1.6 Finance and Accounting

Objective: *Assess the finance and accounting career cluster and understand how the management, measurement, movement, and recording of transactions can put professionals into the highest levels of management.*

Career pathways into finance and accounting lead serious professionals to banking, stock market brokerages, insurance companies, corporations, and audit firms. The business of dealing with money and assets is a crucial part of American enterprise, a profession of high-level challenges and opportunities.

Business Vocabulary

- accounting (p. 34)
- asset (p. 34)
- bond (p. 36)
- business-to-business (p. 21)
- commodities (p. 36)
- communication (p. 28)

- communication media (p. 28)
- continuing education (p. 4)
- diagnostic services (p. 16)
- distribution channel (p. 21)
- e-commerce (p. 10)
- entrepreneurs (p. 24)
- finance (p. 34)

- interactive media (p. 10)
- logistics (p. 23)
- merchandising (p. 22)
- network systems (p. 10)
- portfolio (p. 31)
- retailer (p. 21)

- stock (p. 36)
- therapeutic services (p. 16)
- trade associations (p. 5)
- virtual office (p. 8)
- wholesaler (p. 21)
- wire services (p. 32)

Key Concept Review

1. What are some transferable skills you could develop as you pursue your career? (1.1)

2. What might a career ladder look like in a profession that appeals to you? (1.1)

3. If you went into information technology, would you prefer to be in support services, software, interactive systems, or hardware? (1.2)

4. Which health science career pathways would put you in direct contact with patients? (1.3)

5. Why is continuing education important in health science? (1.3)

6. Where would you find entry-level positions in wholesale/retail sales and service? (1.4)

7. Would you rather work in some areas of logistics, marketing, or retail operations? (1.4)

8. If you went into communication and media, would you prefer that your career ladder include more technical or more creative jobs? (1.5)

9. Why do commercial artists need to have computer skills? (1.5)

10. What is the difference between corporate accounting and public accounting? (1.6)

Online Project

Professional Associations and Certification

Almost every profession and industry has a trade association that supports it, and many offer certification programs. Use a search engine to find associations relating to a career pathway that interests you and list some of the available certifications.

Step Up the *Pace*

CASE A   *Climbing a Career Ladder*

A friend has just retired from a marvelous career that took her from an entry-level position all the way to the top of her profession. Imagine what her career ladder looked like and how she planned her advancement, gained skills, and trained herself, methodically moving up from one job to the next.

What to Do

1. List as many "rungs" as you can think of on the career ladder that might reach to your friend's job. You might want to talk with a career counselor or someone in the profession to give you some ideas.
2. List some skills, education, training, and certification that might have helped your friend advance so far.
3. Now write a one-page biography describing your friend's career.

CASE B   *Transferable Skills*

A friend of yours graduated from tech school and went into the technical side of media broadcasting. He is now a video technician, but he's a little dissatisfied with the job. He wants something that's more personally rewarding. He contacts you because you are a pharmacist in a hospital. He's thinking about getting into health science, so he asks you how someone with his skills could switch careers.

What to Do

1. What jobs in the hospital could your friend qualify for without much additional education?
2. What skills does your friend probably already have that could be used in the health science field?

Research Letter

When considering a career in an unfamiliar field, do your research! After exploring resources in books, Web sites, and personal contacts, consider writing a company to learn additional information. Write to request input about

- Available positions
- An annual report
- Company brochures and literature
- A person in a particular department, such as the human resources director.

If you use the postal service and not e-mail, enclose a self-addressed stamped envelope for the reply. Remember to use the correct letter format, no matter which type of mail you use.

Which format below is the best to use for an inquiry letter?

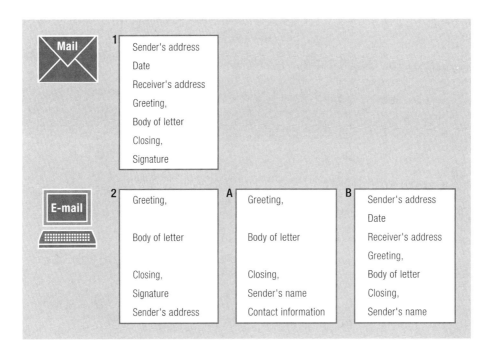

Both #1 and A show the correct formats to use for an inquiry letter. Information such as the sender's address and date are already included on e-mail. Be sure to use the appropriate format for the type of mail you are sending.

Exercise: Choose a form of mail and a type of request you might actually want to make. On the lines provided, write an inquiry letter. Create a name and company, if needed.

_____
_____
_____
_____
_____
_____
_____
_____
_____
_____
_____
_____
_____
_____
_____
_____
_____
_____
_____
_____
_____
_____
_____
_____
_____
_____
_____
_____
_____
_____
_____
_____
_____
_____
_____
_____
_____
_____
_____
_____
_____
_____

Professional Business Protocol

What Will You Do?

2.1 Professional Presence: Dress and Grooming Learn how to understand the culture and dress code of your new workplace.

2.2 Meeting and Greeting Learn how to introduce yourself and others as you lay the foundation of solid business relationships.

2.3 Interacting at Work Recognize the importance of mutual respect in the workplace.

2.4 Business Meals, Business Travel Learn to use the pleasure of a meal to form closer bonds with business associates and to make business trips smooth and productive.

2.5 Business by Telephone and E-Mail Examine the protocol for conducting business through electronic media.

Why Do You Need to Know This?

Corporate culture is the rules, traditions, values, and styles that are unique to each company, just as national cultures are unique to each country.

Corporate culture and business practices vary from place to place and are difficult to define. As you enter into a new workplace, you'll need to assess quickly the corporate culture and learn the written and unwritten rules of behavior. Once you see how people behave in your workplace, you'll want to present yourself so that you fit with the group, and yet stand out as an individual or future leader.

This chapter will show you how to dress for success, how to interact with others in the office and on business trips, and how to communicate effectively with customers and co-workers whom you may never meet in person.

Chapter Objectives

After completing this chapter, you will be able to:

- Dress and groom yourself for success in a job interview and in daily business.

- Meet people and make them comfortable when they talk with you.

- Work well with others without prejudice, sexism, and sexual harassment.

- Mix business with pleasure as you travel and dine.

- Use the telephone and e-mail to do your job efficiently.

Set the *Pace*

You and Your Workplace   Have you ever seen the professional you hope to be—someone in an office or on the street, or even in a movie or on TV? Picture that person at work in his or her office. Think of the clothes, shoes, hairstyle, accessories, and every other detail about that person's appearance.

- What physical details make this person stand out as a good professional?
- What is the person likely to do when someone enters the office?
- Imagine that person on the phone, moving smoothly from saying "Hello" to getting down to business.

Activity   In the journal section of your career portfolio, write a paragraph describing someone you've seen who looks, to you, like the ideal professional. Describe what that person wears and write a sentence or two about his or her grooming style. Then write a paragraph about the person meeting with a sales representative who has just entered his or her office. In a third paragraph, write a phone script in which that person calls the sales rep to place an order, says hello, then smoothly gets down to business.

Professional Presence: Dress and Grooming

Clothes talk. Haircuts talk. Fingernails, shoe polish, tattoos, and pens talk. If they're yours, they're talking about you. With a little care, observation, and planning, you can make sure your clothes, accessories, and grooming are saying nice things about you.

Dress for Your Job. A *conformist* is a person who fits in with the group. You may not like to think of yourself as a conformist, but in the business office, conformity is good. It doesn't mean you're a sheep. It means you're part of a team. If conformity in clothing bothers you, try to imagine Michael Jordan dashing down the court in another team's uniform. With that in mind, think about how you should dress for your job so you fit in as a team member, yet stand out as a future leader.

Look Like What You Want to Be

We may not be aware of it, but we judge others by their clothes. We may assume that an old suit means old ideas, that shabby shoes mean carelessness, and that a tacky tie is the uniform of a different team, one that we don't want to belong to. Similarly, people may assume that the professional who is well dressed and well groomed is also well prepared to do a good job.

Sending Silent Messages

Clothes and grooming send silent messages. Your new suit tells others that you're a natural part of the business world. Your tasteful tie or silk blouse marks you as part of the team. Your well-shined shoes imply that you're ready to get to work. Your well-groomed hair is a gesture of respect to your co-workers.

In other words, you're looking good and you're going places. The attention you've paid to your appearance will pay you back in other ways. That sounds great in theory, but how do you make sure that your appearance is saying what you want it to say?

Business Fashion

Business fashion has undergone a revolution in the past few years. Not so long ago, suits and ties were required of all men, and women needed a burdensome wardrobe of formal business outfits, no matter what their rank in the office.

That formal atmosphere has changed a lot, but not completely and not everywhere. Depending on the business, the region, the occasion, the profession, and the season, today's office attire can range from suit-and-tie formality to jeans and short-sleeve casualness.

Reading and Study Tip

Skimming
Before you read, survey this section to see what you'll learn. Read main headings, lists, captions, and side columns.

" *A diploma from Harvard helps a lot. Lacking that, get some really nice shoes.* "

Anonymous

Dr. Joe Pace
UNDERSTANDING
ORGANIZATIONS

"*Learn how institutions operate. You will be part of an institution or organization for much of your life. Be aware of how it works.*"

Dress Code

A company's **dress code** is a set of rules that determine how employees should (and should not) dress on the job. Sometimes the dress code is written into the **personnel policy,** a written set of rules and information that pertain to working at a given company. Sometimes the dress code may be unwritten and unspoken yet understood by people who work there.

As you begin your new job, you're going to need to learn the dress code and, as quickly as possible, conform to it. Let's start at the beginning—your job interview.

dress code a set of rules that determine how employees should (and should not) dress on the job

personnel policy a written set of rules and information that pertain to working at a given company

Step One: Get the Job

The person who interviews you for your job will be assessing your clothes and grooming almost as much as your diploma and résumé. You want every thread and crease to say that you are a natural fit with the company team; that there is nothing odd about you; that you will never shame the company, scare off a customer, or disrespect your position. Your interviewer should know this about you even before you shake hands or say a word. You will say it all with your clothes.

What She Wears

If you are a woman, wear a well-coordinated outfit.

- A quality, conservative, dark, matching blouse and skirt is most effective. A dress and jacket or suit also would be appropriate.
- Blue, gray, beige, and tan are the best colors. Wear neutral or skin-toned stockings.
- Your jewelry should be minimal, quiet, and almost unnoticeable.
- Avoid spike heels or open-toed shoes.
- A trendy haircut may be seen as reflecting immaturity, so tell your hairdresser you want something neat and professional.
- Your makeup should be subtle and tasteful. Avoid wearing perfume.
- Your nails shouldn't be extravagant works of art, but they should be neat, clean, filed, and perhaps polished with a neutral color.
- No jeans, dangling earrings, bangle bracelets, cheap accessories, political buttons, see-through blouses, bare shoulders, athletic shoes, or visible tattoos.

What He Wears

You want to look businesslike, as well dressed as anyone in the company.

- Suit and tie are always appropriate for an interview, even in offices with a casual dress code.
- Your suit must not look old, out of style, shabby, flamboyant, wrinkled, or ill-fitting. It should be dark blue, gray, or subtle pinstripe, and either new or dry-cleaned.
- Your shirt should be new or cleaned and pressed, and white or light blue.
- Ask someone who knows fashion to coordinate your suit, tie, shirt, socks, and shoes.
- Shoes should be new or newly shined. Loafers and lace-up shoes are fine, but no boots, moccasins, or athletic shoes.
- No earrings or visible tattoos. No more than one ring on each hand.
- Your fingernails should be clean, even, and filed.
- Your haircut should be conservative or stylish without being trendy. Have a barber touch up and trim your beard or mustache.

Interview Dressing Dress well to make a good impression. *Why is dressing conservatively for an interview the best approach?*

- You should wear no fragrance or a very subtle after-shave or cologne. Use a neutral deodorant.
- You should be fastidiously neat and clean, with well-combed hair, spotless eyeglasses, and teeth brushed and flossed.

You Are What You Carry

You'll be judged by not only your clothes but also the "business tools" you carry into the office. Invest in or borrow a good leather briefcase. Load it with extra copies of your résumé on good paper, a business magazine and newspaper, a good pen and sharpened pencils, a legal pad, breath mints, and a comb or brush. Don't carry anything that would embarrass you if seen.

Try to have nothing in your hands besides that attaché case. Leave your right hand free for shaking hands quickly and eagerly. Women should avoid carrying both a purse and an attaché case. Let the latter serve as the former. If you must carry a purse, make it a small one.

Decipher the Code

Congratulations! You got the job. You walked in there looking like a vice president, and the way things are going, you just might become one.

But while you were in there for the interview, what did you notice about your new colleagues? Were the men in pinstripe suits or khaki slacks? Were the women in silk blouses or flannel shirts? What kind of shoes were people wearing? What kind of store sells such clothes? If someone had orange hair in twisted spikes, was it someone in a position you want? Who was the most comfortable and professional-looking person of your gender? *That's what you want to look like.*

Be Cautious with Casual

Some offices allow **casual dress,** that is, clothes a notch less formal than suits. Some offices designate a weekly **casual day,** a day when no one wears suits unless they have an important meeting with people from other companies.

Don't let a casual dress code fool you. Casual *does not* mean old, sloppy, or ragged. It means clean, good-quality, fashionable, well-pressed slacks, shirts, blouses, and dresses. People in a given office have probably quite unconsciously worked out a dress code that may tolerate or prohibit such questionables as jeans, workboots, black shirts, body piercings, bow ties, khaki pants, and sandals. One last thing: Many companies are backing off from the casual dress code. Be alert for what's happening at your company and the companies you visit.

You probably can't go too far wrong by following a few basic guidelines:

- It's better to be overdressed than underdressed. You can adjust later.
- If no one is of suit-and-tie formality, avoid that extreme but consider dressing close to it.
- Dress like those in the upper, not lower, ranks.
- If something about your intended attire bothers you, swap it for something that leaves you feeling confident and comfortable.
- If people are wearing uniforms or shirts with corporate logos, that's obviously what you want to wear. Call the human resources department to ask for details.
- If there's a written dress code, it takes priority.

Watch for Changes

During your first days on the job—in fact, during your first year—you'll want to notice what changes. Does the boss dress differently for meetings with clients and other people from outside the company? When do seasonal changes into sweaters, short-sleeve shirts, boots, or sandals take place? How do others dress when they leave on a business trip? How casual do people really get on casual days?

If you dress well, work hard, and do a good job, before long you may well get a promotion or a transfer to a different department or office. This change in venue may well mean a change in clothes, too. If you're going to a different region, styles may be noticeably different. People in New York, Miami, Dallas, Los Angeles, and Detroit don't dress the same way. Likewise, account executives dress differently from floor managers in the same office. The accounting department may have one dress code while sales has another and marketing yet another. The culture at corporate headquarters differs from that at a manufacturing facility.

Look Good for Meetings

You might also need to upgrade your style for special meetings with the company president or important customers. A business meal may demand better clothes. If you haven't been able to observe such events in advance, don't be afraid to ask someone who has. Aim to be as well dressed as all others present.

New Attitudes / New Opportunities

Dress for Success, an international, not-for-profit organization, helps low-income women entering the professional workforce to acquire appropriate attire. Each woman receives one suit for a job interview and another once she is hired. Here's what Ricki Weiss, the founder and executive director of Dress for Success in Cleveland, Ohio, says about . . .

The Importance of Dressing Professionally   "If you don't dress professionally on an interview, you're not going to get a professional job. Usually, an interviewer has already read your résumé and checked your references. The purpose of an interview is to find out if you can communicate and present yourself well. Dress more conservatively than normal. Avoid anything that is going to distract the interviewer and take attention away from you, like dangling earrings or loud colors."

Professional Dress Once You Are Hired   "Every office has its own culture. If you have an eyebrow ring, take it out for the interview. If you see others there wearing eyebrow rings, then that's probably acceptable. It depends on the job; if you are at an advertising agency, clients may not believe someone wearing a plain suit is creative. You also have to ask yourself: if the culture of a job requires you to dress in a way that you don't like, is that job really for you?"

Some Solutions for People on a Tight Budget   "Everyone should have a white button-down shirt as well as dark pants. The main idea when interviewing is to be neat and clean. Have everything pressed, wash your hair, and carry a nice pen. Interviewers aren't looking at the price tag on your clothes; they are looking at how you present yourself."

Advice on Interviewing from Her Experience   "In an interview, usually you are nervous and don't have time to think clearly. Never decline or accept a job on the spot. As you leave, be sure to shake hands and tell the interviewer you would like to work for him or her. Leave with the impression that you would accept an offer; you can always decline afterwards. Always wear a smile, be positive, arrive exactly ten minutes early, shake hands firmly, and look people in the eye when you speak. Be confident and look the part."

Effective Shopping

Your first job in the business environment—or your new job in a different business environment—will probably call for a trip to a good clothing store. Your objective is to acquire an effective wardrobe. Look at it as an investment in your career.

If you're a little limited in fashion sense, admit it. Get qualified help. Do you have a friend who dresses well? Let that person be your shopping guide. Before you go, you will have to agree on the style of clothes you need. If you can't describe the clothes of the corporate culture at your new workplace, browse through a few magazines that advertise fashion products. Maybe you or your friend can even call someone at the company and ask for a few pointers on style and the kind of store where you can find the right clothes.

Invest in Quality

You don't need to spend a lot of money to dress well. You can find reasonably priced, good-quality clothes at many chain department stores. Watch for sales. Many retail stores tend to have qualified salespeople, or even fashion consultants, who can help you assemble a respectable wardrobe. These stores usually offer charge cards that will allow you to pay over time.

Your Challenge

It's your first business trip. You fly to Des Moines to meet with an important new customer. Your luggage flies to Honolulu. You arrive at your hotel in khaki shorts, a T-shirt, and athletic shoes. The meeting starts in three hours. What do you do?

The Possibilities
A. Call the customer and try to have the meeting postponed.
B. Call the customer's assistant to confirm the meeting and explain the problem.
C. Ask the hotel staff where you can shop for some clothes.
D. Buy new shoes, douse yourself in cologne and deodorant, go to the meeting in your khakis, explain the problem, and apologize profusely.

Your Solution

Choose the solution that you think will be most effective and write a few sentences explaining your opinion on a separate sheet of paper. Then check your answer with the answer on our Web site: **www.mhhe.com/pace.**

The salesperson will need a general idea of the styles you're looking for. You might bring in some pictures from the magazines you have looked through. Point out that you do not need to make a fashion statement. You want to look professional and feel comfortable with what you're wearing.

The salesperson should take the time to really help you. He or she should be conscious of your budget and aware that you need all the elements of a good wardrobe. Let this professional explain why certain socks go with a certain belt and certain tie and which shirts go with which suits.

Pace Points

Take Charge

Send the right signal and prevent incidents of harassment by choosing to wear modest, professional clothing.

Have Clothes, Will Travel

Your work may occasionally take you to other cities, maybe even to other continents. On trips, you will meet many new people for the first time. In each case, you'll have to make that all-important first impression.

Spending the night on an airplane is no excuse for walking into a meeting looking like, well, like you spent the night on an airplane. Here are some tips for arriving in good shape.

- Call ahead to learn the dress code of the office where you're going. Again: It's better to be overdressed than underdressed.
- Use a garment bag to minimize wrinkling. Carry it onboard, if permitted.
- Do not forget items for grooming and hygiene. (Because of tightened security, be sure you don't have scissors, no matter how small.)
- Pack lightly; airlines have strict allowances about the number and weight of carry-ons, partly because of the terrorist attacks on planes on September 11, 2001.
- Arrive in town with enough time to recover from your trip and touch up your personal appearance.
- Conferences and seminars often adopt casual styles, but special dinners and meetings may require more formal attire. Call the organizer to find out.

Grooming

grooming the preparation of your body for a good professional appearance—everything from haircuts to hygiene

Grooming is the preparation of your body for a good professional appearance—everything from haircuts to hygiene. Professionals in the business world need to maintain the highest standards of personal appearance. "Neat and clean" applies everywhere, and a few basic guidelines tend to apply in most offices.

- Men should be clean-shaven or with mustache or beard very neatly trimmed.
- Haircuts should tend toward the conservative, fashionably in style without getting trendy or abnormal. Men's hair should not touch the collar or cover the ears. No ponytails. Women's hair rarely goes beyond the shoulders. Of course, these basic styles can vary a lot with region and type of business.
- Fingernails should be perfectly clean and even in length. Women's should not be too long or elaborately painted.
- Fragrances, including colognes, after-shaves, and perfumes, should be minimal or not used. Use neutral deodorant.
- Women's makeup should be minimal—enough to improve appearance without being noticeable.
- Do not groom in public. This includes combing or brushing hair, clipping nails, and touching up cosmetics.
- Mouthwash or breath mints are helpful. Avoid being seen chewing gum.
- Be ready for emergencies. In your office and travel kit, have a comb, toothbrush and toothpaste, needle and thread, mouthwash, shoe polish, and basic cosmetics.
- Get some exercise. A twenty-minute workout will do wonders for your looks and your spirit. Regular exercise will leave you looking trim and ready for action.

QUICK RECAP 2.1

PROFESSIONAL PRESENCE: DRESS AND GROOMING

In this section, you've seen why it's important to dress and groom for your job. Here's a quick summary of the key points:

- People presume a well-dressed, well-groomed professional will do a professional job.
- You only have one chance to make a good first impression.
- Learn your company's dress code by checking the personnel policy and by observing others.
- Be careful with a casual dress code. Casual dress still requires clean, quality clothes appropriate to your workplace.
- Watch for changes to the dress code and to the codes of other offices and other companies.
- Dress well for special meetings.
- Shop for good clothes in good stores, and ask for help from people who know fashion.
- Your grooming should be neat, clean, conservative, and impeccable.

CHECK YOURSELF

1. List everything you should wear or carry to a job interview.
2. How should your hair, face, teeth, and fingernails look when you go to work?

BUSINESS VOCABULARY

dress code   a set of rules that determines how employees should (and should not) dress on the job

personnel policy   a written set of rules and information that pertain to working at a given company

casual dress   clothes that are slightly less formal than suits

casual day   a day when no one wears formal office clothing unless they have an important meeting with people from other companies

grooming   the preparation of your body for a good professional appearance—everything from haircuts to hygiene

Meeting and Greeting

In the previous section, you learned how to use your clothing and grooming to signal others that you are a good professional and part of your workplace team. Your appearance makes a good first impression.

"It's good to meet you!"   Much of business is a matter of meeting people, gaining trust, and getting down to work. This section will help you use your professional appearance to move from handshake to constructive conversation.

communication an exchange of information by speech, in writing, or in subtle ways such as tone of voice, style of clothes, and gestures of respect

A Matter of Communication

Business is largely a process of **communication**—an exchange of information by speech, in writing, and in subtle ways such as tone of voice, style of clothes, and gestures of respect. Business begins when communication begins. In business, communication tends to have a business objective. The objective of meeting someone for the first time is to introduce yourself, make a good first impression, and move into a constructive business conversation.

Prepare Yourself

Meeting someone in a business context actually begins well before the introductory handshake. Before the shake of the hand and the first words of greeting, people subconsciously evaluate each other. They make preliminary judgments based on clothes, grooming, body language, and other subtle signals.

In a certain sense, you begin making that first impression as soon as you get up in the morning. You take your shower, put on deodorant, and select clothes appropriate for the events of the day. You're looking and feeling good when you arrive at the office or wherever else you're going to work that day. Marvelous! You're off to a great start. You've prepared yourself to make a good first impression.

Introduce Yourself

trade show an event where companies in a given industry present their products or services

Let's say you're working at a **trade show,** an event where companies exhibit their products or services. You are staffing your company's booth, meeting new people all day, showing off your product, impressing your colleagues with your dynamism, and maybe even making new friends you'll keep for years to come.

Here comes someone who looks vaguely interested in your company's products. Your mission: Step out, introduce yourself to a complete stranger, win that person's confidence, and engage in a conversation that is both friendly and businesslike.

Use Body Language

At first glance, the stranger is already inclined to meet you. Your **body language**—body positions and movements that communicate something about you—are open and friendly. You're dressed and groomed like someone who knows how to do business. You're coming toward him not with a club and bared fangs but with a friendly hand extended, a smile on your face, and enthusiasm in your eyes. By your body language, he recognizes you as someone he would like to meet.

Shake Hands

To shake hands, you don't grab his fingers. Rather, press your palm to his and grip his hand firmly but without trying to prove your strength. Look him in the eye. In an upbeat voice, say, "Hello," or "Welcome to WizzCom," and "My name is So-and-So." Then add a little something to get the conversation going: "Great trade show, isn't it?"

> *Be the first to say hello, and sound like you mean it.*
>
> *Anonymous*

He will, of course, return your handshake, and, hearing a question from you, he will probably respond. He might say a standard (and thus comforting) "Pleased to meet you." He might offer his name. If he does, you might want to repeat it to help you remember it: "Jack Smith, good to meet you. Can I show you how our WizzCom Gizmos work?" You've now made the crucial first moves toward forming a business relationship.

What You Did . . .

Let's look at what just happened.

- You started off by looking like a practiced professional.
- You took the initiative, approaching the other person to introduce yourself.
- You approached with the body language of a friendly person.
- Your handshake was firm but not crushing.
- You offered your name and possibly learned the other person's name.
- You offered a bit of small talk.
- Then you got down to business.

Of course, there are a million variations of this introduction process, but in a certain sense, they are all the same. Two human beings meet and move toward a common goal.

What You Didn't Do . . .

Avoid these pitfalls when introducing yourself in business:

- You didn't use slang or street language.
- You didn't wait to be introduced.
- You didn't say something possibly offensive, such as, "You sure look like you've had a hard day!"

Pace Points

Name Game

If you meet someone who gets your name wrong, don't be offended. Don't correct them publicly. You might take them aside and politely spell or pronounce your name for them. The sooner you do this, the less chance there is that the incorrect name will stick.

Stand Up for Yourself

One other thing. When someone enters the room and you need to be introduced, stand up to shake hands. Do this even if no one else does. If someone presents the new person to you, say your name clearly if the presenter did not. If you did not hear or remember the person's name, ask now for it again. Using a new associate's name presents a welcoming attitude.

Introducing Others

When you would like to introduce someone to other people, it's most appropriate to first introduce the person of highest rank. It's also a nice gesture to first introduce someone who's new to your group or whom you know less well, making that person feel more important and confident. Gender does not determine priority.

Exchange Cards

When business people meet, they very often exchange business cards. The reasons are obvious. They want to remember each other's names and know how to contact each other.

The best way to get someone else's card is to offer one of yours. When you take theirs, say, "Thank you." You can ask for a card at any point when it becomes clear that you may want to contact this person again. The only exception would be when the other person is of much higher rank than you. If he or she doesn't hand you a card when you offer yours, drop the subject.

Always keep a few business cards with you—especially in a business setting. Plan on meeting people today, or at the very least, plan on the possibility. Keep your cards in your pocket or readily at hand.

Planning to Meet

Often you have an appointment to meet someone for a specific purpose. It could be a stranger or a long-time colleague. In either case, you want the meeting to yield results. You do several things to prepare:

- You think about the meeting ahead of time.
- You bring not only your business card but all other documentation, samples, information, brochures, and so on, that you need to fully communicate with the other person.
- You give yourself plenty of time to get there.

You'll want to show up on time, maybe even a little early. Again, this might demand a little planning so that you leave point A with enough time to arrive at point B.

Plenty can go wrong between those points, of course: traffic jams, late planes, or a line at the office copier. It happens. When it does, make every attempt to contact the other person to inform him or her of the delay. If the delay is out of your control, you have no reason to arrive all flustered and overheated. For the sake of politeness, give a brief apology and get down to business. In moments like this, you will be glad that you prepared well, that you brought all necessary documents and other materials, that you left a little early, and that you will be able to make this meeting productive even if you arrived a little late.

Whoops!

If you've been living on planet Earth for long, you know that things can go wrong. Hardly a human being has ever lived who hasn't stuck his or her foot into his or her mouth, forgotten somebody's name, or showed up for a meeting an hour late or a day early. Such mistakes are human and inevitable, and they will certainly happen to you in the business world.

Tips From a Mentor

On Meeting and Greeting

If you're a little nervous about introducing yourself to people, try rehearsing the first few things you'll say. A good line to have in mind is the one that comes after the exchange of names. An open-ended question (that is, one that can't be answered with a simple yes or no) is a good way to start a conversation. Here are some lines you can use:

- Did you have a good trip?

- Is this your first time in our new building?

- Is this your first time at WizzCom?

- Can I get you some coffee or something?

- Is there something you're especially interested in seeing here?

- I'm glad you could join us. We have a great program arranged.

- What company are you with?

- What do you do at GE?

- How's business been?

- You're a little early. Can I show you around?

- What brings you here today?

- Has the meeting been productive so far?

- I'm here to answer any questions you might have.

Let it be of some comfort to know that this happens to everyone, and everyone will tend to sympathize with you in your embarrassment. The best thing to do is make a little joke about it, admit your foolishness, perhaps apologize . . . and then just get back to business, leaving your mistake behind. And don't let it happen again.

Stay Cool

Let's say you're giving a presentation to a potential client. By mistake, you refer to this client with the name of a former client . . . a competitor of the people you're talking to. What do you do?

"Whoops, did I say FabCo? I'm very sorry. I meant LafCo, of course. FabCo is out of the picture. Where was I? Oh, yes . . . our marketing plans for this year . . ."

What just happened?

- You made an innocent and forgivable mistake.
- You admitted it.
- You quickly apologized, giving it no more attention than such a slip-up deserved.
- You stayed cool and you moved on.

Let's say you run into someone you haven't seen in several months. You can't remember her name. You need to introduce her to your boss. What do you do?

"Well, hello! How good to see you again. We met at the trade show, right? Your name will come to me in a moment . . ." She understands your plight and says her name. You say, "Yes, of course. I'm sorry. Sally Doe, I'd like you to meet our C.E.O . . ."

What just happened?

- You suffered a common lapse of memory.
- You admitted it.
- You apologized briefly.
- You stayed cool and moved on.

People with Disabilities

disability any physical or mental condition that limits a person's performance

A **disability** is any physical or mental condition that limits a person's performance. We never say that a person "is disabled." Rather, the person "has a disability." Now and then, you're going to meet people who are in a wheelchair, blind, on crutches, or missing a limb. How do you talk or shake hands with a person with these or any other disability?

Be Polite and Sensible

There's no single answer for all situations, but one thing is always true: These people want to be treated like anyone else. The rule of thumb is simply to be polite and sensible and remember that you're both there to do business, not dwell on a health problem.

To talk to a person in a wheelchair, you may remain standing, squat down, or pull up a chair. If the person is accompanied by someone on foot, avoid the tendency to focus your attention and conversation to the person who is standing up. Don't touch the person's wheelchair unless asked to do so.

If the person is blind, you need not make any changes in conversation. Saying something like, "Do you see what I mean?" is in no way insulting. If you reach out to shake someone's hand and discover the person is missing that hand, shake the other if it's offered. A person on crutches might appreciate a pat on the arm instead of a handshake.

The Bottom Line: Be Personable and Professional

The most important rule of meeting people is to simply be a nice person: Respect others as people and present yourself as a professional who wants to do business

Figure 2.1 *Meeting People*

When you...	you should...	so that...
expect to meet people	prepare yourself by dressing and grooming for the occasion	you present an appearance of professionalism.
see a stranger you want to meet	take the initiative by approaching and introducing yourself	you can begin to do business.
approach someone	use your body language to look friendly and inviting	the other person feels encouraged to meet you.
introduce yourself	shake hands, look the person in the eye, smile, and say your name	the other person feels befriended and answers with his or her name.
are going to be late to a meeting	call ahead and explain	others can adjust their schedules.
arrive late	apologize briefly and get down to business	the meeting is productive.
forget a name or say something wrong	apologize briefly, perhaps explain, and get back to business	you can move on to constructive conversation.
meet a person with a disability	treat the person as any other	the person feels comfortable and accepted as a person.

Thinking Critically Meeting a business associate can be like meeting any new acquaintance. *How might you act differently when meeting someone for business rather than social reasons?*

and do it well. You may feel at first like you are play-acting, but, in time, it will come naturally. Read Figure 2.1 for advice that's easy to follow. In any new situation, model your actions and words on another professional you admire.

QUICK RECAP 2.2

MEETING AND GREETING

In this section, you learned how to meet and work with a new person. Remember these handy tips:
• Prepare yourself with a professional appearance.
• Use body language to present yourself as friendly and inviting.
• Take the initiative to introduce yourself with a handshake and your name.
• Apologize for social blunders, then move on to business.
• Treat people with disabilities as you would anyone else.
• Be human and professional.

CHECK YOURSELF

1. How should you prepare yourself for meeting other people?
2. How can you use body language to encourage someone to meet you?

Internet Quest

Research Tools

Visit the Web site of a business. To find one, ask for the business card of an associate or take a card from a store.

List as much information as you can find about the company from the site. Most Web sites have a site map showing all information featured on the site.

BUSINESS VOCABULARY

communication   an exchange of information by speech, in writing, or in subtle ways such as tone of voice, style of clothes, and gestures of respect

trade show   an event where companies in a given industry exhibit their products or services

body language   body positions and movements that communicate something about you

disability   any physical or mental condition that limits a person's ability

Interacting at Work

In the previous section, you learned how to meet people. Now it's time to give some thought to working with people. That's what business is all about. You can count on meeting a great variety as you pursue your career. You don't have to like everybody, but you do have to work with many different kinds of people and keep your workplace relationships on a professional level.

Working with People. In this section, we will look at how people can work together as a team regardless of differences in race, religion, age, gender, and sexual orientation. The better you can work with others, the more you'll get done, the more satisfaction you'll find in your work, and the more likely you will be to move ahead in your career.

A New Era in Business

The business world has entered a new era. Women are an integral force in the workplace. Racism, sexism, and sexual harassment are considered intolerable.

Companies and competition have gone global. Corporate hierarchies have shifted. People do business via phone and e-mail with people they may never meet face-to-face. Office workers work at home. The self-employed work in offices. Dress codes have changed. Everything is moving faster.

However, some things have not changed. People still need to communicate if they want to get things done. They still appreciate courtesy and respect. They want to know what they should and should not do. They want to know when they've done a good job. They want to do their jobs and make some money. They want to relax and spend time with their families or friends.

It isn't always easy to work well under the ever-changing circumstances of modern business; but because businesspeople share certain goals and values, they manage to get things done. Those who work well together get the most done.

Civil Rights

As you move through the business world, you will meet all sorts of people. Since business is *always* a matter of people working together, you'll succeed only to the extent that you combine other people's skills with yours. Assuming that someone is less capable because of gender, race, religion, sexual preference, or disability will limit your own capabilities.

Equal Treatment Is the Law

Depending on your level of responsibility in a company, prejudice and sexual harassment—or even failing to prevent them—can get you into serious professional trouble, or even legal trouble. Company personnel policies usually state that all persons are entitled to equal treatment and opportunities. (Even if they don't, the law

---

Reading and Study Tips

Opposites

Find an example in this section that illustrates an opposing relationship.

---

does.) Your company policy also may explain what should be done in cases of apparent prejudice or harassment.

Avoid Prejudice and Harassment

prejudice an attitude toward other people based on nothing more than their race, religion, gender, age, or any other characteristics that have nothing to do with their abilities or behaviors

harassment the needless or even unconscious tormenting of other people with improper criticism, inappropriate jokes, sexual pressure, ethnic slurs, or humiliation

Prejudice is an attitude toward other people based on nothing more than their race, religion, gender, age, or any other characteristics that really have nothing to do with their abilities or behaviors. **Harassment** is the needless or even unconscious tormenting of other people with improper criticism, inappropriate jokes, sexual pressure, ethnic slurs, or humiliation. Prejudice and harassment are not only illegal but also just plain bad for business.

Watch for Unconscious Prejudice

Some people have prejudices they do not know they have. You should make it a habit to assess your feelings and actions for signs of prejudice. Ask yourself these questions:

- Do you ever catch yourself assuming that the man in the group is in charge and that the woman is his subordinate?
- Do you ever assume a person's age, race, or appearance is an indication of his or her capability or honesty?
- Are you less likely to talk with a person who has a physical disability?

Pace Points

Sincerity
A sincere apology puts you on the moral high ground.

You owe it to your co-workers, your company, and yourself to look for and curb any such tendencies. If you accidentally say something that could be taken as racist, sexist, or otherwise offensive to someone, the best thing to do is apologize briefly and sincerely, then put the incident behind you and get back to business. In the name of decency and better business, the offended person should accept the apology and say nothing more about it. If harassment or prejudice continues or seems intentional, report it.

Defend Yourself

Though the world has become a lot more conscious of the pains caused by prejudice, a few people haven't gotten the point yet. They still think that everyone of a given race, gender, age, or ethnicity shares the characteristics of a stereotype.

No one at any workplace should have to suffer prejudice. If you think you've been disrespected in this way, it's usually best to say something that lets the other person know that it happened and that you didn't like it. Ideally, a simple comment such as "That wasn't funny" or "What makes you think I'm like that?" will be enough to elicit an apology and stop the offensive behavior.

Resolve the Problem Peacefully

Try to put a stop to the offensiveness by directly addressing the person. If it cannot be resolved quickly, politely, and peacefully, do not raise the level of confrontation. *Never resort to violence or even an implied threat of violence.*

Report the Problem to Management

If the offenses continue and seem serious, check your company policy for the appropriate actions. You should inform your manager. If for some reason you're reluctant to discuss the problem with that person, go up to the next highest level of management. You also can go to the human resources department. If you have to skip over your immediate boss, be prepared to explain why.

Document Incidents

You should document the incident. To **document** something means putting it in writing, noting the date, time, place, circumstances, and people involved. The report should be factual, specific, and complete. Keep a copy of the incident report and give a copy to the appropriate manager. The manager is required by law to do something about your complaint.

Remember: You have a right to get respect and fair treatment. If possible, resolve problems at the lowest possible level of confrontation, preferably at a level that has no future repercussions for anyone.

document to put in writing, noting the date, time, place, circumstances, and people involved

Sexual Harassment

When people work together all day, they can sometimes become attracted to each other. This is normal, and many loving relationships have blossomed in business offices. As long as the relationship is mutually satisfying, it does not necessarily conflict with anyone's career.

Two Kinds of Sexual Harassment

Sexual harassment includes

1. any kind of pressure to become intimately or socially involved, or
2. exposure to any kind of sexually oriented talk, jokes, messages, pictures, descriptions, humiliation, or references to sexual differences between men and women.

Romantic attraction between co-workers can become a problem if one of the individuals is not interested. When one person's suggestions or advances become too insistent, courtship crosses the line to sexual harassment.

sexual harassment (1) any kind of pressure to become intimately or socially involved; (2) exposure to any kind of sexually oriented talk, jokes, messages, pictures, descriptions, humiliation, or references to sexual differences between men and women

No Means No

Asking someone to go out after work is perfectly acceptable, but insisting is not. A firm "no" should put an end to it. If you're the one doing the inviting, take the hint and downshift your relationship to "strictly business."

Pace Points

Impolite But Right

If you are receiving "harmless" but unwanted attention from a co-worker, don't be too polite to speak up. Better to risk hurt feelings and make yourself clear than to let the problem escalate.

Keep It Clean

Some people are easily (and rightfully) offended by jokes that humiliate a given type of person, such as ethnic slurs. Also, many people dislike talk about sex and consider it humiliating or insulting. Displays of pornography will almost always lead to trouble.

Keep your office clean. Don't talk about sex. Don't make jokes about types of people. Don't distribute jokes or pornography via e-mail, and if you receive any material by e-mail, delete it immediately and perhaps warn the sender that you do note appreciate such correspondence.

Report Sexual Harassment

No one should have to tolerate sexual harassment on the job. If romantic advances become annoying, or if you are repeatedly offended by off-color jokes, you should take action to stop it. Your first step toward resolution might be to privately tell the offender that you do not welcome the advances or that you find the jokes crude, offensive, and unbusinesslike. If the problem continues, document your complaint in

Your Challenge

Somehow, your e-mail address has ended up on a list that receives dirty jokes every morning. They come from someone you work with, someone with whom you need to be on good terms. He thinks the jokes are only funny, not offensive, but sometimes the jokes really disgust you. Which of the following actions is most appropriate?

The Possibilities

A. Just delete the e-mail without reading it.

B. Reply to the e-mail to tell the person that the jokes are stupid and disgusting.

C. In a private conversation, politely tell your colleague that you don't appreciate receiving jokes like that because they're offensive and take up your time.

D. Copy some of the jokes and send them to your boss by e-mail, with a note explaining why they bother you.

Your Solution

Choose the solution that you think will be most effective and write a few sentences explaining your opinion on a separate sheet of paper. Then check your answer with the answer on our Web site: **www.mhhe.com/pace.**

a written memorandum to the offender. If that doesn't do it, send a copy of that memorandum plus a detailed explanation to your supervisor.

Sometimes, sexual harassment is unintended, so try to defuse the situation at a confidential and personal level. This will avoid consequences that can cause long-term tension and anger.

Favoritism

favoritism special treatment or privilege given to an employee for reasons that have nothing to do with work performance

Favoritism is special treatment or privilege given to an employee for reasons that have nothing to do with work performance. Favoritism often stems from family ties or friendship. Sometimes the reason is romantic or sexual. Even a mutually satisfying relationship can lead to accusations of favoritism from other colleagues.

Your company's personnel policy may have guidelines regarding relationships between people working at different management levels. The person at the higher management level may have to be very careful to avoid inappropriate decisions regarding assignments, promotions, salaries, and so on. Decisions will have to come with documented justification.

R-E-S-P-E-C-T

Fundamentally, we avoid prejudice and harassment in the office out of respect for our co-workers. That respect extends to the rules and courtesy of the interpersonal activity that we call "doing business." By respecting colleagues, you help everyone remain friendly, cooperative, and productive.

Here are eight ways to show respect for your colleagues:

1. **Be courteous.** An act of courtesy is an act of respect. Words like *please, thank you, I'm sorry, excuse me, nice job,* and *good morning* all tend to mean the same thing: *I respect you.*

2. **Respect privacy.** Personal territories are often cramped in today's offices. Generally, everybody's workspace—be it a cubicle, a suite, or just one desk among many—is open to view. Office doors tend to remain open, except for temporary purposes of privacy or confidentiality.

   Despite this physical openness, people naturally like to think of their workspaces as personal territory. Entering someone else's space uninvited or unannounced can cause a certain uneasiness. A little tap on an open door or the frame of a cubicle is a gesture of respect. Over time, you might develop enough of a rapport with your colleagues that you can freely drift in and out of each other's space, but don't presume you have the privilege until it becomes obvious.

   When someone is not in his or her office space, it is normally acceptable to enter for a moment to place something on a desk. Be aware, however, that going into someone else's desk or files is an intrusion serious enough to cause hard feelings and even accusations.

3. **Don't interrupt.** Avoid breaking in on a meeting, or even a conversation, unless you have a problem that just can't wait. Don't expect people to stop a phone conversation to talk with you. When someone is talking to you, listen. Unless invited to join the conversation, back up to a discreet distance or leave and check back in a few minutes.

4. **Be on time.** Everybody's got work to do. Everybody's got a schedule to keep. Making the effort to show up on time is not only efficient but also respectful.

5. **Don't gossip.** Don't bad-mouth. Don't backstab. Offices breed so much gossip that it sometimes seems like part of the job. It isn't. It's unproductive, often dangerous, and always about someone who isn't present to confirm or deny the rumor.

   As a part of your office community, someone will inevitably deliver a rumor to you. If it sounds like something that has nothing to do with business, you're best off bowing out by saying something firm but polite, such as "I'd rather not talk about other people." Avoiding gossip is good business and demonstrates respect to others.

   Backstabbing is talking about someone or taking actions that hurt others for purposes of self-promotion. It is the ugliest sort of disrespect. It has a way of backfiring and certainly does nothing to help people work together. If you have a gripe against someone, work it out in a professional manner. Either talk to that person or discuss it honestly with a manager. Try to find a win-win resolution that doesn't hurt anyone's reputation.

6. Respect the chain of command. Companies have a **chain of command**—the ranking or hierarchy of employees. This system of reporting and supervision channels information upward and downward through a company. Information flows two ways:

   - Downward from corporate leaders through various levels of management to subordinates.
   - Upward from subordinates through supervisors to upper management.

   When you join an organization, management will make it clear to whom you report and who reports to you. You report to the person who gives you assignments and oversees your work, who is normally the same person to whom you report results and problems. If it's not clear where you fit into

chain of command the ranking or hierarchy of employees that constitutes a system of reporting and supervision that channels information upward and downward through a company

the chain of command, find out. You can create problems for yourself if you report a problem or situation to the wrong person, or accept an assignment from the wrong person.

7. Know the protocol. **Protocol** is a code of conduct that determines, among other things, how people address each other.

Once you know who your boss is, you need to quickly learn how to address him or her. In some companies, first names are fine. In others, the last name is used for managers. In others, first and last names are used. Sometimes Mr. or Ms. is required. Miss and Mrs. have generally fallen from use, but follow people's preferences. In memos and correspondence, you can't go wrong using the person's full name, perhaps with an abbreviated first name, as in G. Washington.

Respect this protocol. Unless the chain of command is very informal in your office, you will almost always communicate in writing only to those immediately above and below you. Only when the person immediately above you fails to take essential action should you go over his or her head. When you must do that, tell the person to whom you're reporting your concern that you are concerned about skipping the chain of command and explain why it is essential that you do so.

8. **Respect yourself.** No one has the right to require you to take on more work than you can handle. No one has the right to make you afraid. No one has the right to treat you unfairly.

You have a right to dignity. If for any reason you feel you are not being respected at work, you have the right to take action. Follow these steps:

1. Document the problem.
2. Report it to the appropriate person.
3. If that person does not solve the problem, go higher up the chain of command.
4. Document every step you take and every obstacle you encounter.
5. In the absolute worst-case scenario, after you have exhausted every possible alternative, go outside the company for legal help.

Getting the Job Done

You're at work to get a job done. Being productive means working with a team, working with discipline, and working for the benefit of your company. Following a few simple rules will help you stay productive, enjoy the cooperation of your colleagues, and be valued (and rewarded) as an employee.

1. **Communicate.** Repetition is better than lack of clarity. Studies show that we sometimes need to hear things at least eight times.
   - Report what you've done, are doing, and plan to do.
   - Remind others about their involvement.
   - Confirm that you've received messages.
   - Alert others to problems.
   - Answer your e-mail.
   - Return phone calls.
   - Use memos to keep people aware of what's going on.
   - When you're out of the office, check in regularly.
2. **Stick to business.** Avoid letting other people distract you.
   - Politely escape from chatty people who tie you up in long conversations.
   - Steer meetings back on track.
   - Avoid personal phone calls and, if you must make a personal call, always keep it short.
   - During idle moments, plan.

3. *Stay organized.* Be prepared and ready to respond.
   - Keep bits of information—phone numbers, appointments, dates, and so on—in a notebook rather than on scraps of paper.
   - Develop an effective filing system.
   - Start (or end) your day with a checklist of things to do.
   - Confirm things in writing.
4. **Help and be helped.** Without overburdening yourself, offer to help colleagues when they have too much to do. Remember: You're part of a team. Never say, "That isn't my job." When you need help, ask for it.
5. **Avoid annoying others.** Offices tend to be close "living quarters." Try to avoid annoying people with music, loud phone conversations, personal chitchat within earshot of others, and other kinds of noise. Avoid messiness and clutter. Avoid interrupting others. Don't eat food where others can smell it or hear you chewing. Don't wear overwhelming fragrances.

QUICK RECAP 2.3

INTERACTING AT WORK

How you treat others professionally can vitally affect how successful you are. As your career advances, remember that the following statements always hold true:

- Everyone has a right to equal respect.
- Avoid prejudice and harassment.
- Avoid jokes and conversation about sex and sexual differences.
- Report harassment to management.
- Be aware that office romance can lead to accusations of harassment or favoritism.
- Respect your co-workers by communicating, helping, and sticking to business.

CHECK YOURSELF

1. What's the first thing you should do if you've been offended by an ethnic or sexual joke?
2. When would you report a problem to your boss's superior?

Check your answers online at **www.mhhe.com/pace.** *Pace* ONLINE

BUSINESS VOCABULARY

prejudice   an attitude toward other people based on nothing more than their race, religion, gender, age, or any other characteristics that have nothing to do with their abilities or behaviors

harassment   the needless or even unconscious tormenting of other people with improper criticism, inappropriate jokes, sexual pressure, ethnic slurs, or humiliation

document   to put it in writing, noting the date, time, place, circumstances, and people involved

sexual harassment   (1) any kind of pressure to become intimately or socially involved; (2) exposure to any kind of sexually oriented talk, jokes, messages, pictures, descriptions, humiliation, or references to sexual differences between men and women

favoritism   special treatment or privilege given to an employee for reasons that have nothing to do with work performance

chain of command   the ranking or hierarchy of employees that constitutes a system of reporting and supervision that channels information upward and downward through a company

protocol   a code of conduct that determines, among other things, how people address each other

Business Meals, Business Travel

Business trips and business meals are great ways to meet people and get to know them better. At some point in your career, you'll probably have to travel to see clients, attend conferences, visit branch offices, or work with co-workers in other cities. You'll also be having lunch or dinner with co-workers, getting to know them as you "break bread" together.

Productive Meals and Trips. In this section you will learn how to mix business with pleasure as you dine with business associates. Business meals call for a certain **etiquette**—the rules of politeness and courtesy that are a lot like the ones your mother taught you, but modified for business relationships. This section also gives you hints for more productive business trips.

etiquette the rules of politeness and courtesy that include table manners, limits of conversation, and other appropriate behavior in public

Some General Advice

If you travel for business, you're going to need a credit card—preferably one of the better-known ones. Most hotels and rental car agencies require the use of a credit card. Obviously, credit cards are also very useful in unexpected situations. You might consider having one or two cards that you use exclusively for business expenses. Keep in mind that most employers will require receipts for reimbursement of your expenses.

You'll need receipts for all your expenses. Keep them organized. When you can't get a receipt or forget to ask for one, note the amount, the reason, the date, and the place.

Get in the habit of working while traveling. Always look and behave your best, even where you think you'll never be recognized. Always carry business cards, a pen, a pad, and a watch.

Pack for Success

Packing is a science. Get a book that describes how best to do it, or search the Internet for "How to pack a suitcase." Your main objectives are to arrive with (a) everything you need and (b) clothes that don't look like they live in a suitcase.

- A garment bag will minimize wrinkles.
- Think about what clothes you'll need for various events.
- Put your shoes in a plastic bag. Place heavy and bulky items along the spine of the suitcase.
- Fold jackets inside out to minimize wrinkles.
- Isolate liquids (shampoo, etc.) in plastic bags.
- Develop a checklist of things you always take on business trips.
- Take an emergency kit that includes needle and thread, cold and allergy medicines, shoe polish, and so forth.
- Call your hotel to see if there will be a clothes iron in your room. If not, take a small iron designed for travel.

Pre-Flight Tips

Trips by plane can be comfortable and productive if you plan them well.

- Make a list of what you must remember, including photo identification, tickets, work documents, cell phone, agenda, personal data assistant (PDA), and phone numbers.
- If you're going to travel by plane, someone in your office will probably handle the flight and hotel reservations. If not, a travel agency can save you time and trouble.
- Missing a flight can really mess up your business mission. Arriving at the airport early isn't a waste of time if you bring work with you.
- Dress as you would at the office, or better. You are always representing your company, and you never know whom you will meet on the plane or in an airport.
- Make a "To Do" list for your trip. Airplanes and airports are good places to read and write reports, prepare for meetings, and organize information on your laptop. You can't use your cell phone on the plane, so make your calls at airports.
- Between flights, always call your office.

In-Transit Tips

Travel time doesn't have to be a bother—it can be very constructive.

- If you plan to work on the plane, business class will give you the elbow room you need to get things done.
- If you have special dietary restrictions, the person who books your flight also can request a special meal.
- You can probably get on the plane even if you forget your ticket; but if you forget your photo ID, you're not going anywhere except back home to get it.
- When passing through the security check, do NOT make any jokes about hijacking, hostages, bombs, terrorism, or any such topics. The security officials really will arrest you.
- Alcoholic beverages worsen jet lag. If you're crossing time zones, drink lots of water instead.
- Secure identification to your suitcase. Don't depend on stickers to stay stuck.
- A ribbon or something else unique tied to your suitcase handle will help you identify your luggage at the airport. It also helps prevent someone from taking your suitcase by mistake.

Have a Nice Drive

When preparing to drive your car on a business trip, start by knowing where you're going. Take a map. Prepare for traffic jams. Also:

- Be sure the car is clean, inside and out, including the trunk.
- If you rent a car, rent one that your client will feel comfortable in.
- Reserve your rental car as early as possible. When there's a big conference or trade show in town, the good cars can be booked well in advance.
- Pack your suit and shirts in a garment bag that you can hang in the car.
- Dress as you would in the office, or better. Neckties are worn outside the seat belt.

- In some states, it's illegal to use a cell phone while driving, and in all states, it's a risk best avoided, especially if the road is unfamiliar. Pull over so you can focus on the conversation and easily access documents. Headsets can also be handy.

Checking In

At your hotel, make yourself at home. Unpack as soon as your arrive. Hang up your clothes or put them in drawers. Iron wrinkled clothes. You may have visitors, so keep your place neat and organized.

Call your office to check for messages, to advise them where to reach you, and to take care of business. During your entire trip, keep checking in. Call the person you'll be visiting to confirm your meeting. Resolve any last-minute details about your business. Consider suggesting a meal together. Food and drink consumed at the hotel can be charged to your room, thus simplifying your expense report. However, beware: your bar tab will appear there, too.

Use Your Concierge

concierge a hotel employee, usually with a desk in the lobby, whose job is to help guests solve problems and get around town

Good hotels have a **concierge** whose job is to help guests solve problems and get around town. The concierge can help you find a dry cleaner, recommend a good restaurant, give you a schedule of local events, help with the local language, and offer other kinds of help.

The Etiquette of Eating Out

Eating together is a ritual as old as civilization. Business meals are one contemporary form of this gesture of sharing, friendship, and generosity. It's a unique opportunity to become closer to your clients, customers, partners, colleagues, and other business associates.

Conversation should be interesting, but light and nonthreatening, as seen in Figure 2.2. If you're doing the inviting, you also should make the reservation and expect to pick up the check. This is especially true when inviting a client or customer.

Getting Down to Business

Pace Points

See Food

Remember your childhood lessons at a business meal: Don't talk with your mouth full!

If you arrive before the other people, wait at the entrance for a reasonable time. If they still haven't arrived, have a seat at your table, but refrain from ordering until you're sure the other person isn't coming. If the person then arrives, stand up, shake his or her hand, and apologize for starting without them. When the meal begins, be sure to follow the rules of etiquette noted in Figure 2.3.

Save the business talk for later in the meal, ideally after the main dish has been cleared. If you need to take notes, don't forget to bring a small pad and a pen or your PDA. If you're bringing folders and other documents, keep them in a briefcase under the table until after the meal.

Paying the Check

If one person has clearly invited the other, the host should pay. Men are not necessarily expected to pay when dining with women. If you're there with a client or customer, make every effort to pay. If you want to pay for the meal, be the first to reach

Figure 2.2 *Good Conversation*

Conversation can include every topic of interest to those involved—with a few exceptions. Here are a few Do's and Don'ts:

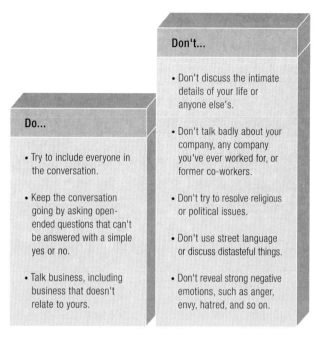

Do...

- Try to include everyone in the conversation.

- Keep the conversation going by asking open-ended questions that can't be answered with a simple yes or no.

- Talk business, including business that doesn't relate to yours.

Don't...

- Don't discuss the intimate details of your life or anyone else's.

- Don't talk badly about your company, any company you've ever worked for, or former co-workers.

- Don't try to resolve religious or political issues.

- Don't use street language or discuss distasteful things.

- Don't reveal strong negative emotions, such as anger, envy, hatred, and so on.

Thinking Critically Even if the other people at the table seem to want to hear gossip, don't—the long-range effects could hurt your career. *What topics of conversation are acceptable at a business luncheon?*

Figure 2.3 *Rule of Thumb*

A crowded table often causes confusion over which glass or bread plate is yours. Use this rule of thumb: look at the thumb and index finger on both hands. The left hand fingers form a letter *b* and the right hand fingers form the letter *d*. Remember that the left-hand *b* stands for the bread plate on your left; and the right-hand *d* stands for the drink on your right.

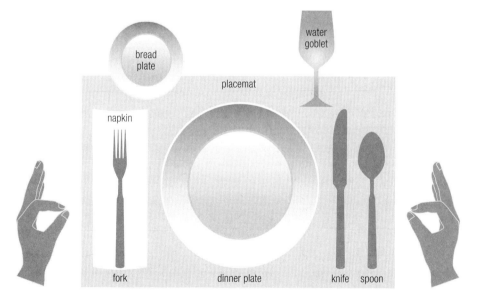

Thinking Critically Your napkin is set to the left of your plate. *Create a trick to remember which napkin is yours.*

Tips From a Mentor

Rules of Etiquette

When enjoying dinner with others in a business setting, keep these important rules of etiquette in mind.

- Turn off your cell phone, pager, beeper, etc.

- Don't hold the chair for women. That's the wait staff's job.

- After everyone is seated, place your napkin in your lap.

- Don't eat until everyone has been served.

- If you drop a napkin or utensil on the floor, leave it there and ask the wait staff for a new one.

- Avoid food that will be difficult to eat with a knife and fork, such as spaghetti, lobster, and chicken with bones.

- If you absolutely must get up from the table, do so between courses.

- Cut one piece of food at a time, shifting the fork to your left hand as you hold the knife in your right.

- To eat your bread, tear off a bite-sized piece, butter it, and eat it.

- Eat calmly and quietly, with closed mouth.

- Remove unwanted food from your mouth with a fork. Don't spit it onto your plate or into your napkin.

- Drink less alcohol than anyone else at the table.

- When you're done, place knife and fork parallel on your plate.

- Avoid picking your teeth in public.

for the check. Expect a little resistance. Insist that your company wants to cover it. Likewise, when someone else picks up the check, offer to pay or to split the total. Don't take too much time discussing the check, however. Give in to insistence and express your thanks, perhaps mentioning that next time, your company treats.

Dining in Someone's Home

If you are ever invited to your employer's or to a customer's house for a meal, here are some helpful hints to keep in mind.

- Bring a small gift such as flowers, chocolates, or a bottle of wine for the host and hostess.
- Make sure you let them know ahead of time if you have dietary restrictions, for medical, religious, or personal reasons. Most people are

happy to oblige and won't be offended if you can't eat something they've prepared.

- The same goes for holiday parties. If you're invited to a Christmas party and you're not Christian, accept the invitation as a social engagement. If absolutely necessary, explain that you don't actually celebrate the holiday.
- Respect your hosts' home and property. They are inviting you into their personal space, so be mindful of their privacy. Don't go wandering around unless invited to do so.
- Sending a thank-you note to the hosts is always appreciated and always a good idea.

International Travel

International travel is always interesting and usually not as risky or tricky as some people may think. Use it as an opportunity to expand your understanding of the world and its cultures. If you get the opportunity to travel out of the country, congratulate yourself on a career that is really taking you places!

Passports, Please

Your **passport** is issued by your own government and will identify your nationality when you travel. You'll need one to enter most countries (including your own) and to get on an international flight.

passport a document issued by your own government that identifies you and your nationality

If you don't have a passport, get one now. Government security checks can cause unexpected delays. American citizens can download the passport application form from http://travel.state.gov/download_applications.html. Non-Americans should contact their nearest consulate.

Many countries require a **visa,** an official permission to enter the country, usually stamped in your passport. Contact the appropriate consulate or the embassy in Washington, D.C., or in a nearby major city. The consulate may be able to fax you the forms or direct you to a Web site. You will have to send them your passport and possibly some photos. Do so by overnight delivery and request the same in return. Some consulates can do this in three days, but it can take as long as three weeks. Your passport also could be lost in the process. Consider having a travel agent handle this task. Few, if any, countries require proof of vaccinations. Consulates can confirm their requirements.

visa official permission to enter the country, usually stamped in your passport

Language

English is today's universal language, but that doesn't mean that everyone speaks it. Don't expect that. Business people and hotel personnel will usually know enough English for their professional purposes, but police, taxi drivers, and shop owners may not.

If you have trouble communicating:

- Be patient.
- Enunciate clearly.
- Speak in short sentences.
- Use your hands.
- Smile a lot.
- Write difficult words so the other person can read them.
- Don't count on electronic translators for anything but basic phrases.
- Express thanks when someone agrees to speak your language.

A pocket-sized phrase book may be more useful than a dictionary. You can go a long way with *Please, Thank you, Where is, How much, I want, I'm sorry, Excuse me, I don't speak (the local language),* and *Do you speak English?* A few local phrases tossed into your English conversation will indicate your good intentions. Handshakes and smiles say the same thing in all languages. Don't leave home without them.

If you need an interpreter for your business meetings, your business contact should provide one unless you're there for a sales presentation. In that case, ask the local company whether they'll need an interpreter. Offer to cover the cost, but ask them to make the arrangements.

Be Aware

Defense against crime is the same in other countries as it is in American cities. Keep your wallet secured and don't keep all your money and credit cards in one place. Leave your passport in the hotel and carry a copy. If threatened, don't resist. The hotel concierge or your local business associate can warn you about especially dangerous areas.

However, don't let fear of crime or terrorism keep you imprisoned in your hotel. Explore a bit of this new corner of the world. Accept (but don't expect) invitations to homes and places of interest. Take a look at the local newspaper to determine local business issues.

Clothes

Formal American business attire is acceptable in all countries. Don't try to adopt the apparent informality of locals unless you really feel comfortable doing so. (Sometimes seeming informality has a lot of fashion style behind it.) Rural and manufacturing locations can be a lot less formal. In most Middle Eastern countries, women are expected to dress very modestly. Check a travel book or ask a travel agent for specific advice. Obviously, you will also have to consider the local climate.

QUICK RECAP 2.4

BUSINESS MEALS, BUSINESS TRAVEL

Sharing meals with clients and traveling to customers can help business, but only when done well. Remember this advice when planning to travel or eat with a business associate.
- Plan to work while you travel.
- Use credit cards.
- For flights, don't forget photo identification and, if necessary, passport and visas.
- Keep yourself, your car, and your hotel room neat and clean.
- Make reservations for everything: flights, rental cars, hotels, and restaurants.
- Keep meal conversation friendly but not too personal. Discuss business, not politics or religion.
- Offer to pick up meal checks, especially for clients.
- Save all receipts for expense accounts.

CHECK YOURSELF

1. List five productive things you can do while traveling.
2. How should you plan to present business information during a meal?

Internet Quest

Plan a Route

Practice using online maps and location finders to get driving directions, times, and distances.

Find weather and road conditions for your hometown or a travel destination. Go to www.mhhe.com/pace for links to online maps.

BUSINESS VOCABULARY

etiquette   the rules of politeness and courtesy that include table manners, limits of conversation, and other appropriate behavior in public

concierge   a hotel employee, usually with a desk in the lobby, whose job is to help guests solve problems and get around town

passport   a document issued by your own government that identifies you and your nationality

visa   official permission to enter the country, usually stamped in your passport

Business by Telephone and E-mail

It's simply amazing how much of today's business is conducted by e-mail and telephone. Professionals often do business with others without ever meeting face-to-face. This new reality of the global/electronic business world makes it all the more important that you be able to present yourself well by phone and e-mail.

Over the Wire. In this section, you will learn to use the phone and e-mail as effective tools that help you get work done. You will find out how to make your phone calls efficient and productive. You will learn some of the etiquette involved in the use of conference calls, speaker phones, and cell phones. You will see how e-mail can be used to communicate ideas precisely and keep information organized.

Reading and Study Tips

Example Sample
Find a paragraph on this page that includes a statement followed by examples.

Phone Manners

When you talk with someone face-to-face, you use a variety of communication tools. Your words, the tone of your voice, your body language, and your ability to read someone's face for indications of whether they understand and accept what you're saying all work together to help you deliver your message.

Over the phone, however, you're limited to words and tone of voice. It's hard to know whether the person you're talking to is scratching his or her head in confusion or nodding with understanding.

Words and voice are your main "telephone tools." You can strengthen them several ways.

- Remember that *hello* and *good-bye* are as important as *please* and *thank you,* even with people you know well.
- When closing a conversation, a sincere and friendly thanks for a person's ideas or time will leave the person glad they talked with you: *"Hey, Bob, thanks a lot for all the information and your time. I really appreciate it. Take care. Good-bye."*
- By consciously modifying the tone of your voice, you can make the other person feel good about talking with you. People like to talk with people who sound happy, enthusiastic, interested, gung-ho, and generally upbeat.
- Just using such upbeat phrases as "Wow!" and "Great!" and "I'm glad to hear that!" will actually make your voice sound more enthusiastic.

Answering calls

If you're receiving calls for the company as a whole, answer with the name of the company. Find out if your company has a certain phrase it prefers to use. If the call is coming to your own phone, answer with your name and perhaps your department. If you're answering someone else's line, say so. Be sure to speak slowly and clearly; although you may have said the phrase hundreds of times, the caller may be hearing it for the first time. See Figure 2.4 for suggestions on how to phrase a phone greeting.

Figure 2.4 *Phone Phrases*

Answering for your department, you can say	If you're answering your direct line, you can say	If you're answering someone else's direct line, you can say
"Marketing Department, may I help you?"	"Joe Wislowski."	"Jane Busch's line, Max Granger speaking."
"Marketing Department, this is Janice."	"Joe Wislowski speaking."	"Hello, this is Jane Busch's office; this is Max."
"American XYZ, Marketing Department, may I help you?"	"Hello, this is Joe Wislowski."	"Hello, this is Jane Busch's office, Max Granger speaking."
"Marketing Department."	"Marketing. Joe Wislowski speaking."	"Hello, this is Jane Busch's office, may I help you?"
"Marketing. How may I direct your call?"	"Joe Wislowski. May I help you?"	"Marketing Department. May I help you?"

Thinking Critically Callers may want the information given in a greeting to know if they have called the correct person. *What do you do with a caller who needs to speak with someone in a different department?*

Know Your Phone

Modern phones are packed with features. If you know how to use your phone, it is a powerful tool. If you don't, it can be a source of frustration and embarrassment. Study the instruction manual. You should know how to

- Put a call on hold.
- Transfer a call to another phone.
- Make a **conference call** involving three or more telephones at different locations.
- Use the speakerphone.
- Record a voice mail announcement.
- Check your messages from another phone.

conference call a phone call that includes people at three or more locations

Prepare for Calls

It helps to prepare for a phone call you are about to make, just as you'd prepare for a meeting.

- Jot down an agenda for the call. List the main points you must remember to discuss.
- Try to know what you're going to say before you have to say it. Rehearse a few sentences or questions that you'll have to deliver. You need the right words and the right tone of voice. This is especially important for challenging phone calls such as sales pitches and calls delivering bad news.
- Be ready with your information. Have all the files and documents you'll need to keep the conversation efficient and productive. Avoid having to put someone on hold. Anticipate questions that may be asked of you.

- Have pen and paper handy for taking notes. You might want to jot things in a notebook that always stays on your desk.
- Have your appointment calendar at hand.
- Close the phone call by summarizing what you've discussed and specifying who's to do what. Don't forget to say thank you and good-bye.

Leave a Good Message

voice mail a system that allows a caller to leave a message for a person who does not answer the phone

Today's offices are very dependent on **voice mail,** a telephone message system that lets callers leave messages on individual phones and lets people call in to their own phones to hear their messages.

In the course of doing business, you're going to have to leave a lot of messages. Good messages are packed with useful information, including

- Your full name and phone number.
- The reason you called and what you'd like to know.
- The date and time you called.
- When the best time would be to call back.

Don't assume that your message got through. If you don't get a return call in a reasonable time, call again. Also, consider sending the message by e-mail or leaving it with an assistant.

Your Message Announcement

The announcement you leave in your voice mail for callers should make them glad they called.

- Keep it concise. Avoid such redundancies as "I'm not able to take your call right now."
- Give your name and possibly your company or department.
- When necessary, give an alternate name and phone number for urgent calls. (And advise that person to expect calls.)
- Don't say anything cute or humorous.
- Speak in a clear and enthusiastic tone. Listen to yourself and re-record your message if necessary.

Screening Your Calls

It's quite acceptable to screen your calls when you have a project to finish or you're in a meeting. Let voice mail or a co-worker take a message for you. If you're not ready for the probable caller, it might be best to pass up the call, prepare yourself, and call back when you are ready.

Remember: when you miss a call, return the call as soon as possible. When you do, it's not necessary to explain why you missed the call. At most, "I'm sorry I missed your call" will suffice. If you get "caught" screening your calls, have a good reason!

When your phone rings, you may want to hesitate for a second before answering. Ask yourself:

- Who might be calling? What do they expect to hear from you?
- Are you ready with pen and paper?
- If you're talking on the phone and hear a "call-waiting" tone, do you really want to put your current caller on hold to attend to the incoming call?

- If you're busy with something, should you let your voice mail take a message?

Speaker Phones

Never use your speakerphone to place a call. Call with the handset, then ask permission to use the speakerphone. Unless necessary for a group conversation, don't use the speakerphone with someone of higher rank. When using the speakerphone, close the door to your office to avoid distracting others.

Cell Phones

Using a cell phone in any crowded place is likely to irritate a lot of people. You might also end up broadcasting confidential information. If you must use a cell phone in a public place, keep it short and quiet or take the phone to another room. Never let anyone hear you mention someone's name or the name of a company, especially yours. A good rule of thumb is: Never use a cell phone in a place where you wouldn't sing.

Conference Calls

Conference calls enable people in three or more locations to engage in one phone conversation. To set up a conference call, you will need to call all of the participants, putting each on hold while you call the others.
Conference calling requires special etiquette.

- First, know what you're doing before you start organizing the call. Cutting people off by mistake is annoying and inefficient.
- Call people according to their rank or importance, starting at the bottom.
- As you contact each person, say, "Hello, this is Jack, lining up a conference call with Gladys. Are you ready? Please hold while I call the others."
- When everyone is connected, introduce everyone to the most important person. Give each person a chance to say, "Hello, Gladys," to confirm the connection and the audibility of each voice.
- Until everyone's voice is recognizable, say "This is Jack" before you speak.
- Don't forget to say good-bye to everyone, and when appropriate, thank people for their time and participation.

Calming Angry Callers

Depending on your position in the company, you may receive calls from people who are angry. Generally, they're angry with your company or its product, not at you. Still, it's only human for them to direct their anger toward the person who's answered the phone.

Remember: Your company's main business is to keep customers happy. That is your objective. If the anger is a relentless onslaught, it might be best to let the person lose steam before you react. If you find an opportunity to interrupt the person and solve his or her problem, do so politely. Saying "I think I can solve your problem" will do much to calm the caller, but only if it's true. Speak in a calm and encouraging voice as you tell the caller how you can help.

If you need to transfer the call to someone else, say something like, "I know who can help you. Hold for just a second while I transfer you to (someone or some department)."

Pace Points

Passing the Buck
With angry callers, do whatever you can to address their complaint. Only connect them to another person if you genuinely can't help.

Don't Argue

Above all, don't get pulled into an argument. Don't raise your voice. Don't say anything aggressive, such as, "No, now you listen to me . . ." If the caller interrupts you, listen politely. Express sympathy without admitting undeserved guilt or error. Say things like, "I understand how you feel" or "Let's see how we can solve the problem."

Don't Suffer Abuse

You want to calm and help an angry caller, but that doesn't mean you have to suffer vulgarities, threats, or other abuse. Warn the abusive caller that he or she must calm down so you can help them. If the abuse continues, warn that you're going to have to hang up. Document the incident, writing down the reason that you had to terminate the call. Report any threats of violence.

Closing a Complaint Call

In closing a call, thank the caller for reporting the problem. If it hasn't been solved, explain what action you're going to take. If you may need to contact the caller again, get a name and phone number. Don't forget to say "Good-bye." See Chapter 3 for more tips on handling customer complaints.

You've Got E-mail

e-mail written messages that are sent from computer to computer over an office network or the Internet. Typically written as *E-mail*, *email*, or *e-mail*

E-mail is a system that allows people to send written messages from one computer to another over the Internet or an office network. See Figure 2.5 for more key facts about using electronic mail.

E-mail has few definite rules, but four principles always apply:

1. Always respond as soon as possible, even if only to confirm that you have received a message. Your confirmation can simply be the word *confirmed* or *noted* returned with the original message.
2. You don't need to respond to copies of messages that were sent to other people unless it's to correct incorrect information.
3. Keep the message clear, concise, and correct.
4. Be professional in language and emotion. Remember: Your message can be forwarded and copied around the world at the speed of light.

Write Well

A well-written message can solve or prevent problems, but a poorly written message can cause problems. Follow these guidelines:

- Use simple words and simple sentences.
- Use standard grammar and spelling.
- Write nothing extra, but leave nothing out.
- Reread and revise it before you send it.
- Informal language is usually acceptable, but avoid slang, gossip, vulgarity, trendy expressions, dirty jokes, and sexual innuendo. Do not use too many abbreviations.

Figure 2.5 *Advantages and Disadvantages of E-mail*

Electronic mail, or e-mail for short, is a relatively new tool in the business world.

E-mail...	so...	but...
is in writing	it's easy to confirm what you said later	you can't deny what you said.
can be forwarded widely and instantly	it's easy to communicate with others on your team	the message may be forwarded to unintended persons.
can be carefully thought out and made perfectly clear	the reader will understand exactly what you mean	your reader will assume you meant what you wrote, even if it's wrong.
lets you carefully choose your words	you can express your feelings well	written words do not allow you to use your tone of voice to express your feelings.
can be permanent	you can refer to it later	it is easily deleted or lost.
can be deleted anytime (before being sent)	you can get rid of anything you're sorry you wrote	if you sent it, you never know if it still exists somewhere.

Thinking Critically All companies can monitor all e-mail in any company computer. *How should you handle a personal e-mail from a friend or family member while at work?*

Use the Power of E-mail

E-mail applications offer features that make it a powerful tool. Use them well and apply these suggestions:

- Use "**reply**" to keep a record of your e-mail dialogue. Clicking "Reply" sends your response along with the message that you received, reminding the sender of what was discussed.
- Use "**cc**" to keep people informed. Addressing people in the "cc" box tells them that they are receiving a copy. (Originally, *cc* stood for "carbon copy.")
- Use "**bcc**" to prevent other people's names and e-mail addresses from appearing in your e-mail. Clicking "bcc" will send your message to other people without listing their names and addresses. (Originally, *bcc* meant "blind carbon copy.")
- Use "return receipt" to automatically give you confirmation that your message has been received or opened.
- Use "**forward**" to send someone a message that you have received. (You will still have a copy in your own "In Box.")

Be Careful!

E-mail is not private. Companies have the right to look at it. Don't write anything that would cause you embarrassment if others were to see it. See Figure 2.5 on the advantages and disadvantages of using e-mail.

> *The best business plans are straightforward documents that spell out the "who, what, where, why, and how much.*
>
> *Paula Nelson*
> U.S. Economist

reply an e-mail feature that sends your response along with the message that you received, reminding the sender of what is being discussed

cc an e-mail feature that sends a "carbon copy" of your message to other people, who will know they are receiving a copy

bcc an e-mail feature that sends a "blind copy" of your message to other people without listing their names and addresses

forward an e-mail feature that lets you send someone a message that you have received

Professional Business Protocol

Acting professional means following business protocol, or a code of conduct, in any way having to do with your job. Protocol includes everything from how you dress to how you communicate to how you eat at business meals. Try to follow the standards discussed in this chapter when working in and out of the office. In following protocol, you help advance your job towards a successful career.

QUICK RECAP 2.5

BUSINESS BY TELEPHONE AND E-MAIL

Phones and e-mail are integral means of communication in business. Communicate more effectively by following these guidelines:
- Know how to use the features on your phone.
- Prepare for your phone calls.
- Provide useful information when you leave a message in voice mail.
- Create a good, professional announcement in your voice mail.
- Remain calm and polite with angry phone callers.
- Always respond to the phone messages and e-mail you receive.
- Use e-mail effectively by writing well.

CHECK YOURSELF

1. How can you prepare for an effective phone call?
2. How can you make e-mail effective and safe?

Check your answers online at **www.mhhe.com/pace.**

BUSINESS VOCABULARY

conference call   a phone call that includes people at three or more locations

voice mail   a system that allows a caller to leave a message for a person who does not answer the phone

e-mail   written messages that are sent from computer to computer over an office network or the Internet; typically written as *E-mail, email,* or *e-mail*

reply   an e-mail feature that sends your response along with the message that you received, reminding the sender of what is being discussed

cc   an e-mail feature that sends a "carbon copy" of your message to other people, who will know they are receiving a copy

bcc   an e-mail feature that sends a "blind copy" of your message to other people without listing their names and addresses

forward   an e-mail feature that lets you send someone a message that you have received

Chapter Summary

2.1 Professional Presence: Dress and Grooming

Objective: Learn how to understand the culture and dress code of your new workplace.

In this section, you learned how to dress so that your clothes tell others that you are a serious business professional. Dressing your best for an interview, then conforming to the office dress code once you get the job, is an important part of your approach to a career. It's helpful to shop for clothes with someone who knows fashion. You also learned that grooming should be conservative and low-key.

2.2 Meeting and Greeting

Objective: Learn how to introduce yourself and others as you lay the foundation of solid business relationships.

In this section, you learned to dress to impress people you've never met before. Introduce yourself with confidence and friendly conversation, then get down to business. Offer your card and expect one in return. To prepare to meet people, know your stuff and take your materials. Keep cool if you've made a mistake. Apologize briefly, leave it behind, and move on. People with disabilities need no special treatment when you meet them. They expect the same respect you give others.

2.3 Interacting at Work

Objective: Recognize the importance of mutual respect in the workplace.

This section focused on ways to respect the equality of all people. You learned why it's important not to cross the line between courtship and sexual harassment or to tolerate harassment of any kind. Respect your colleagues. Be on time; don't gossip. Offer help, and respect the chain of command. Try to resolve conflicts peacefully and privately, but report to management if necessary. Get the job done by communicating with others, keeping yourself organized, sticking to business, and cooperating with your colleagues.

2.4 Business Meals, Business Travel

Objective: Learn to use the pleasure of a meal to form closer bonds with business associates and to make business trips smooth and productive.

In this section, you found out how to use business meals to become better acquainted with your associates. The many travel tips suggested that you give yourself plenty of time to catch planes, and so forth, and that you dress well when you travel. Learn to pack a suitcase so that you arrive with clothes in decent condition. During business meals, observe basic table manners, avoid heated discussions, and pick up the check when appropriate (especially when you're with a client).

2.5 Business by Telephone and E-mail

Objective: Examine the protocol for conducting business through electronic media.

This final section prepared you to be polite and professional on the telephone. You learned to use your voice to convey a positive attitude and leave messages that bring you results. When dealing with complaints, calm angry callers. Try to solve their problems if possible. Be careful with e-mail: It can spread beyond your control. Keep e-mail formal when contacting people for the first time. As with everything you write, edit e-mail to make it clear, accurate, and concise.

Business Vocabulary

- bcc (p. 83)
- body language (p. 57)
- casual day (p. 51)
- casual dress (p. 51)
- cc (p. 83)
- chain of command (p. 67)
- communication (p. 56)
- concierge (p. 72)
- conference call (p. 79)
- disability (p. 60)
- document (p. 65)
- dress code (p. 49)
- e-mail (p. 82)
- etiquette (p. 70)
- favoritism (p. 66)
- forward (p. 83)
- grooming (p. 54)
- harassment (p. 64)

- passport (p. 75)
- personnel policy (p. 49)
- prejudice (p. 64)

- protocol (p. 68)
- reply (p. 83)
- sexual harassment (p. 65)

- trade show (p. 56)
- visa (p. 75)
- voice mail (p. 80)

Key Concept Review

1. How do you dress well and groom appropriately for a job interview? (2.1)

2. What is the best way to dress for everyday work at your office? (2.1)

3. If you don't have "clothes sense," what's a good way to select clothes to add to your wardrobe? (2.1)

4. When you introduce yourself to someone you don't know, who should be the first to offer a handshake? (2.2)

5. How should you introduce a person whose name you've forgotten? (2.2)

6. What's the best way to hold a conversation with someone in a wheelchair? (2.2)

7. What are some ways to show a gesture of respect to your co-workers? (2.3)

8. In what situation would you most likely pick up the check after a business lunch? (2.4)

9. How do you best prepare for a phone call? (2.5)

10. How do you leave a useful phone message? (2.5)

Online Project

Netiquette

Type these keywords into a search engine of your choice and see what you come up with: **e-mail etiquette.**

From your search results, pick five sites that address the issue of e-mail etiquette or online protocol. Review each site's suggestions and write your own list of top ten e-mail etiquette rules. Share them with your class.

Step Up the *Pace*

CASE A   *Helping a Friend in Need*

Your buddy from tech school, Antoine, is from another country. He's learned English fairly well, but he doesn't dress very professionally. You assume this is because the style of professional dress is different in his country than it is here. He's going to a job interview at a software design company, where he hopes to get an entry-level position in research and development. He needs some help with his wardrobe but doesn't have much money.

What to Do

1. Write a list of ways he might stretch his budget to buy clothes for the interview.
2. Write a paragraph or two about where you would take him to shop and what kind of clothes you would suggest he buy.

CASE A   *Dealing with Unproductive Co-workers*

You've just landed a job scheduling incoming and outgoing shipments at a trucking company. The office is comfortably informal, but the managers tend to be absent from daily office business. Many employees take advantage of the lack of supervision. They come in late and take long lunch breaks. They sit around talking even when they have work to do. They spend a lot of time with personal telephone calls. They swap raunchy jokes. You want to take your job seriously, but all the fooling around distracts you. Meetings are unproductive because people arrive late, leave early, and chat about personal matters.

What to Do

1. List some of the ways you can maintain your self-respect and professionalism in this environment.
2. Write a paragraph or two telling what you could do to encourage better work.

Percentages

Here are two ways to calculate a percentage discount. Which one do you think is easier?

Both options involve two steps. You have to decide which option makes the most sense to you: finding the amount of discount then subtracting it from the original amount (Option 1) or finding what amount is left after the discount (Option 2). The answer will be the same no matter which option you choose.

	Step 1	Step 2	Answer
Option 1			
To calculate 20% off of $65.00, multiply $65 by 0.20. This equals $13. Now, subtract $13 from $65 to determine the discounted price.	$65 x .20 ――― $13	$65 − $13 ――― $52	$52
Option 1			
To calculate 20% off of $65.00, subtract 20% from 100% to find the percentage of the original amount left. Then, multiply $65 by .80, or 80%.	100% − 20% ――― 80%	$65 x .80 ――― $52	$52

Tipping

Calculating a tip can be a nightmare if you're not comfortable with math, but there is an easy way to figure out a good tip.

If you want to tip 20%, start by calculating 10%. If your bill is $15.00, move the decimal point one place to the left to give you 10%. 10% of $15.00 is $1.50. Now, double that to get 20%. $1.50 times 2 equals $3.00. 20% of $15.00 is $3.00.

For 15%, do the same thing but only add half to your 10%. For example, 10% of $20.00 is $2.00. Half of $2.00, or 5%, is $1.00. 10% plus 5% equals $3.00, or 15%.

A quick way to calculate 15% of a tab is to check the tax listed on your bill. If you are in a state where the tax on food is 7.5% (0.075), then just double the tax to calculate 15%. For example, if the tax on a $20.00 bill is 7.5%, it will be listed as $1.50. Double that to get $3.00, or 15%.

Exercise: On the lines provided, calculate the total bill for the following situation:

You have a meal in a restaurant where the chef prepares the wrong order for you. After you send it back, it takes 15 minutes to get your proper order. The manager offers you 20% off of your bill to make up for the inconvenience. You still want to tip your waitress 15% of the original total because she was very nice and helpful while you were waiting. The original total for your meal without 20% off is $35.50.

Develop a Customer-First Attitude

What Will You Do?

3.1 *The Importance of the Customer* Gain an understanding of what a customer is and how to recognize what customers need and want.

3.2 *Understanding Advertising and Public Relations* Study the importance of corporate identity, logos, and brand names and how to use these identities to appeal to customer needs, attitudes, and lifestyles.

3.3 *Interacting with Customers* Learn how to use attitude and language to cultivate customer loyalty and respect.

3.4 *Managing Customer Complaints* Become familiar with the principles of help desks, call centers, and tech support networks and how they are used to help customers.

3.5 *Interacting with Internal Customers and Suppliers* Understand how the people with whom you work in your company are your customers and suppliers.

Why Do You Need to Know This?

Your company's most important person isn't the president, the CEO, or the chairman of the board. It's the customer. Your company exists to satisfy customers, and ultimately, everything you do is aimed at that all-important objective.

Satisfying your company's customers involves a lot more than just handing them a product or providing a service. You need to recognize who can use what you offer. You need to help them remember that you and your company are there to help them. When there's a problem with your company's product or service, you need to resolve the problem and retain the customer's goodwill. This chapter will teach you how to take care of your company's most important person.

Chapter Objectives

After completing this chapter, you will be able to:

• Recognize potential customers and how you can help them.

• Use your company's reputation as a sales tool.

• Approach customers, satisfy their needs, and solve their problems.

• Deal constructively with customer complaints.

• Manage employees involved in customer service.

Set the *Pace*

The Customer-First Attitude Customers aren't just the people eating in restaurants and shopping in stores. They are plumbers who need gaskets, corporate managers who need auditors, and radio stations that need advertisers. Pick three companies at random from the Yellow Pages of a telephone book. Imagine who their customers are by thinking about these questions:

• What kinds of people does each company have as customers?
• How would each company introduce its products to potential customers?
• How would employees in the human resources, information technology, or maintenance departments serve their companies' customers even though they don't work with them directly?

Activity Would you like to have a good professional clean your home, top to bottom, tomorrow? Of course you would . . . . but you probably won't. List three or four reasons why hiring a cleaning service would not be appropriate for you at this time. Perhaps you live in a small apartment or are on a tight budget. Then, for each reason, write a line of dialogue that a cleaning service sales representative might use to get you to change your mind.

The Importance of the Customer

When you think of selling, do you envision doors slammed in your face, people getting annoyed as you try to persuade them to buy what they don't want, or angry customers storming back with products that didn't work right? Well, relax. Your relationship with customers will be nothing like that. With the right attitude on your part, the customers you serve will see you as someone who is dedicated to helping them and making their lives better. By helping them, you can make them glad to do business with you.

Know Thy Customer. Everyone in business has the same job: to satisfy customers. To do that, you need to understand your customers—who they are, what they need, and what they expect when they buy a product or pay for a service. The customer comes first, and the best way to put the customer first is to *know* the customer.

❝ *It's not just important to be friendly and courteous to the public, it is essential.* ❞

Disneyland Trainers
As Cited by Arnold Sanow, Business and Marketing Expert

customer a person who needs or wants products and services

need in the business sense, everything from outright necessity to realistic desire

The Customer Comes First

Satisfying the customer is the ultimate purpose of any company. It makes sense, then, that the customer has top priority. Serving the needs of the customer is more important than closing the store on time; more important than your own personal convenience; more important than answering the phone, stocking the shelf, or punching the clock. *The customer comes first.*

Needs and Wants

All customers have one thing in common: They are human beings, and all human beings are **customers**—people who need or want products and services. **Needs** include food, shelter, warmth, and security. However, people also want and seek status, comfort, convenience, entertainment, information, beauty, and education.

Not everyone needs what a company provides. However, many more people might need it or want it if they knew about it and realized how it could make their lives better. By understanding your customers, you can get an idea of their needs. Once you know their needs, you can work to satisfy them.

Needs Are Not Simple

Customer needs can be complicated. Consider this situation: Harry Doe walks into a fast-food restaurant. He wants a cheeseburger, a soda, some French fries, and a little extra ketchup. That's all he orders, but what does he expect?

- He expects food that is safe to eat.
- He expects the cook to know how to prepare the food.
- He expects decent treatment from the person at the counter.
- He expects service in a reasonable amount of time.

- He expects a clean table.
- He expects a clean restroom.
- He expects a proper response if he complains about a cold cheeseburger.
- He expects the same quality of food and service he got the last time he ate there.
- He expects the same quality of food and service that was advertised on TV.

The lesson here? Your company is never just selling an isolated product or service: It is providing customers with support and commitment.

Support and Commitment

Support refers to your company's efforts to ensure that the customer is satisfied with the product even long after it's purchased. At the restaurant, support includes the clean restroom, the extra ketchup, and the manager who will listen to and resolve complaints. At the computer manufacturer, support includes the technical support desk that customers can call, the supply of spare parts, and the line of peripherals and accessories.

Commitment is your company's seriousness about delivering what it promises—and more. It's the training of the cook, the 100-percent beef in the cheeseburger, and the effort to serve the French fries hot. It's the latest technology in the computer chips, the promise to fix a broken product even after the warranty expires, and the extra effort to pack the product well before shipment. Customers don't necessarily think about support and commitment when they buy a product, but when support and commitment are missing, customers soon notice.

support a company's efforts to ensure that the customer is satisfied with the product long after it is purchased

commitment a company's seriousness about delivering what it promises—and more

Products and Services

Some companies provide products, from food to electricity to computer chips. Some companies offer services, from preparing French fries to delivering electricity to installing software. Many companies offer combinations of products and services, such as car dealers that offer cars and car maintenance, electronics companies that offer radar systems and training, and retail stores that offer furniture and interior design.

Sometimes it's hard to tell product from service. Harry Doe paid for not just a cheeseburger but also for the service of preparing it. He also paid for the training of the cook, the cleaning of the restroom, and the certainty that he was eating safe food.

Dr. Joe Pace
SERVICE

"No one has ever risen to spiritual maturity until he has found it finer to serve someone else than to serve himself."

What Does Your Company Really Sell?

Sometimes companies have a deeper insight into what they offer the customer. A manufacturer of hammocks, for example, might see that it is really offering comfort and relaxation. A lawn care service might see itself as offering homeowners free time. By understanding what your company is *really* offering its customers, you can more effectively communicate with them and satisfy their needs.

❝ The exact words that you use are far less important than the energy, intensity, and conviction with which you use them. ❞

Jules Rose
Vice President, Sloan Supermarkets

Customer Demographics

Demographics are the characteristics of a group of people—their ages, incomes, average incomes for each age bracket, average number of cars per household, and so on. Companies study demographics to identify who in the general public might have a need for their products. People who live in apartments, for example, have little need for lawn mowers but may need laundry detergent in small boxes. If your

demographics the characteristics of a group of people—their ages, incomes, average incomes for each age bracket, average number of cars per household, and so on

Myth: Selling is mostly about products or services.
Fact: Selling is mostly about knowing the customer's needs.

company sells lawn mowers, it will want to identify people who own houses in sub-urban areas.

Even though you may not be analyzing demographics in your job, you should always remember that certain types of people need certain types of products and services. As you talk with customers, arrange product displays, plan seasonal sales, coordinate marketing efforts, and so on, you should be thinking of the demographics of your potential customers. Matching customers with products will help you think about the different needs of customers with different life circumstances.

Study the demographics of three American consumers. Which is the best potential customer for each product?

Potential Customers
- **Harry Fentwirth:** male, 28, married, two children (5 and 8), household income $28,000, lives in rural Georgia, owns three-bedroom house, two cars.
- **Phyllis O'Shay:** female, 67, widowed, lives alone, household income $23,000, lives in Miami, rents studio apartment in senior housing complex, no car.
- **Carmen Degas:** female, 42, married, no children, household income $122,000, lives in Philadelphia, owns a condominium, one car.

Products
- Lawn seed spreader
- Laptop computer
- Fishing tackle
- Gas furnace
- Window flower boxes
- Matching luggage
- DVD player
- Internet service
- Inexpensive sneakers
- Pet products

Study the demographics of three American consumers. Which is the best potential customer for each product?

Thinking Critically Each potential customer has different demographics. *Which products might be important to all three customers? Why?*

- Organic breakfast cereal
- Life insurance
- Housecleaning service
- Taxi service
- Snowshoes
- Tickets to a Minor League baseball game
- A train ticket to New York
- Picture frames

Trends Are New Opportunities

Society and business are always changing. Consumers develop needs for new products and preferences for new styles. Businesses look for new technologies that give them a competitive edge. Change often comes in the form of trends. New trends create opportunity. If a new trend seems to appear suddenly, it's only because you didn't see it coming. In reality, trends start small but quietly snowball as people catch on. To serve your customers better, watch for trends. See them as opportunities.

Retail Trends If you're in retail, you'll want to know what styles and products are becoming more popular. You can find out by doing several things:

- Monitor sales to detect changes in customer preferences.
- Watch movies and television programs to see what products actors are using.
- Pay attention to advertisements to look for new products and see how styles are changing.

Industry Trends If your customers are other companies, be attuned to what's happening in the industry you sell to:

- Study **trade magazines** (publications that are produced for particular kinds of businesses rather than for consumers) to look for industry news and new products.

trade magazine a publication produced for a particular kind of business rather than for consumers

Trade shows events where companies in a given industry present their products in booths

- Attend **trade shows** (events where companies in a given industry present their products in booths) and notice what's changing in products and services.
- Talk with your colleagues and customers to know what's happening in new products and technology.

QUICK RECAP 3.1

THE IMPORTANCE OF THE CUSTOMER

- When interacting with customers, your main goals are to learn the customer's needs and to satisfy them.
- Customers need more than the products they buy. They need the company's commitment and support.
- By knowing a customer's demographics, you can have an idea of what the customer needs or doesn't need.
- Trends create new opportunities to satisfy customers.

CHECK YOURSELF

1. What do we mean by a customer's "needs"?
2. What does a customer need besides a company's product?

Check your answers online at **www.mhhe.com/pace.**

BUSINESS VOCABULARY

customer   a person who needs or wants products and services

need   in the business sense, everything from outright necessity to realistic desire

support   a company's efforts to ensure that the customer is satisfied with the product long after it's purchased

commitment   a company's seriousness about delivering what it promises—and more

demographics   the characteristics of a group of people—their ages, incomes, average incomes for each age bracket, average number of cars per household, and so on

trade magazine   a publication produced for a particular kind of business rather than for consumers

trade shows   events where companies in a given industry present their products

Understanding Advertising and Public Relations

Your company probably puts a lot of effort into presenting its products to potential customers. Advertising and public relations make people aware of a product. Your company may send catalogs to potential customers to get them to buy its products. Stores may hold special promotions for your products. The purpose of these and other marketing efforts is to present your company's products in the best possible light.

Help Your Products Help Your Customer. Your customers need to know about your company's products. They need to know what those products are, what's so good about them, and how they can help make lives better. If you work in marketing, your job is to know your products, know who needs them, and know how to introduce them to each other.

The Process of Presenting the Product

As a professional in your company, you may well be involved in the process of presenting products to customers. You may interact with them face-to-face in a sales or assistance situation. You may work behind the scenes in advertising or public relations. Wherever you are in the process, you need to understand how companies present their products and services to the public.

Sell the Image

When customers consider buying a product, they consider not only the features of the product but also the **image** that comes with it, the idea that the public associates with the product. Many people who buy SUVs, for example, don't necessarily need off-road capability. They want the image of the adventurous person who would need an SUV. They need the image more than they need four-wheel drive.

You, as a representative of your company, are part of that image. If customers perceive you as friendly, knowledgeable, helpful, and professional, they will have a better image of your company. If you present yourself well, customers will be all the more eager to consider your products.

Your Company's Brands

When customers choose among several products, they tend to look for brands they admire and trust. A **brand** is a unique name given to a company's product. The brand name is usually a **trademark**—a word or phrase that is registered with the government so that no one else can use it. Brand names come with reputations and images. Sometimes customers want the brand name as much as the product itself. Think of clothing you've seen with the brand name boldly displayed. Sometimes that brand is represented by nothing more than its **logo,** a symbol that represents the brand or its company. McDonald's golden arches, the Macintosh apple, and the Nike swoop are three famous logos.

Reading and Study Tips

Compare and Contrast
To compare means to find similarities. To contrast means to find differences. Compare and contrast the role of advertising departments with the role of public relations departments.

image the idea that the public associates with a product

brand a unique name given to a company's product

trademark a word or phrase that is registered with the government so that no one else can use it

logo a symbol that represents a brand or its company

Marketing

marketing all the business activities that present the product, its brand, its image, and its reputation to the customer

Marketing is all the business activities that present the product, its brand, its image, and its reputation to the customer. Marketing puts the product on the shelf, the car in the showroom, the order form in the magazine, and the "click here to order" button on the Web site.

Much of marketing is purely psychological: putting the product in an attractive package, increasing the brand awareness and logo recognition, and helping the public to associate the brand with a certain image. This is accomplished by putting the image of the product in front of the customer.

Whatever your position in a company, from sales rep to vice president, it's important that you be aware of the company's marketing efforts. You want to know the products, the images, the brands, the logos, the recent sales and promotions, and so on. You want to know what the customer is looking for and what they have seen and heard about it.

Advertising and Public Relations

advertising a commercial message that appears in a space or time slot that has been paid for by the advertiser

media all the means of communication that can present an advertisement to the public, such as magazines, newspapers, television, radio, and billboards

public relations a marketing effort that tries to put a company and brand name in view of the public without actually buying space or time slots

Companies cannot depend on word of mouth to inform the public about products. Therefore, they use advertising and public relations to communicate with the public. See Figure 3.1 for some of the advantages and disadvantages of using advertising and public relations in marketing.

Advertising is a commercial message that appears in a space or time slot that has been paid for by the advertiser. Advertising appears in **media,** which can be defined as all the means of communication that can present an advertisement to the public. Among advertising media are print media, such as magazines and newspapers, and broadcast media, such as television and radio. Other media include billboards, signs on the roofs of taxis and the sides of buses, posters in the windows of stores, Web sites, e-mail, and direct mail, which sends advertising directly to possible customers at homes and businesses.

Public relations, or P.R., is a marketing activity that puts company and brand names in view of the public without actually buying space or time slots. This is accomplished by feeding information to reporters, sponsoring special events, and placing products and brand names in prominent locations. For example, a drug company may give a magazine editor information about a product that can help prevent a certain disease that can be treated with the company's product. By sponsoring an event such as a concert or marathon, a company hopes to have its name mentioned in the press.

Figure 3.1 Advertising vs. Public Relations

	Advantages	Disadvantages
Advertising	Company can carefully craft the message. Company can place the message in specific places and time slots in the media.	Lacks credibility due to obvious company bias. It's expensive to repeat the message in a full advertising campaign.
Public Relations	More credible than advertising because it is generated by the media, not the company. Less expensive than advertising.	Company cannot precisely specify the message. Company cannot guarantee appearance of message in the media.

Thinking Critically Advertising and public relations are alike and different. *Why do companies use both advertising and public relations in marketing?*

Returning Resolutions

Your Challenge

You work at the service desk for a retail store. A customer wants to return an item bought last month. Your store, however, has a 30-day return policy. It has been longer than 30 days since the customer bought the item, so you cannot offer a refund. What do you do?

The Possibilities

A. Tell the customer that he or she should have brought it back sooner, and now he or she must keep the item.

B. Tell the customer that the store has a stupid policy, but you must uphold it.

C. Give the customer a refund if they complain.

D. Offer store credit for the value of the item.

Your Solution

Choose the solution that you think will be most effective and write a few sentences explaining your opinion on a separate sheet of paper. Then check your answer with the answer on our Web site: **www.mhhe.com/pace**.

You, Marketing, and the Customer

If your company's advertising and public relations efforts are successful, customers will want to buy your products. Customers will

- Recognize your brand names.
- Assume that brands they recognize are of superior quality.
- Associate brand names with images.
- Know about sales and promotions.
- Be more willing to learn more about the product.
- Go along with a trend that marketing has inspired.

It is important for you to pay attention to your company's marketing efforts so that you

- Know your company's brand names.
- Know what products your customers are looking for.
- Know the images your customers associate with those products.
- Help the customer appreciate the products.
- Know about sales and promotions.
- Are able to foresee trends.

You Are Your Company

You are an important part of your company's public relations effort. If you deal directly with customers, they will associate you with your company. If they see a well-dressed, well-groomed, polite, friendly, helpful, knowledgeable employee, they may unconsciously assume that your company is professional and honest and is selling a good product. If you provide services only to others in your company, or

Pace Points

The Little Things

Tell customers about deals, refill empty water glasses, remember personal details, foresee needs. Sometimes the "little things" make the biggest difference!

internal customers, remember that your efficiency and professionalism contribute to the image of the company. By keeping your internal customers satisfied, you help make the company and its products look good.

QUICK RECAP 3.2

UNDERSTANDING ADVERTISING AND PUBLIC RELATIONS

- Know your company's marketing efforts and your product's image so you know what the customer is looking for in your products.
- Advertising and public relations will prepare customers to consider your products.
- Let your company's marketing efforts back you up when you present products to customers.
- To the customer, you *are* your company. Your professionalism makes your company look good.

CHECK YOURSELF

1. What are the differences between advertising and public relations?
2. How does a company's marketing effort help you help your customers?

Check your answers online at **www.mhhe.com/pace.**

BUSINESS VOCABULARY

image   the idea that the public associates with a product

brand   a unique name given to a company's product

trademark   a word or phrase that is registered with the government so that no one else can use it.

logo   a symbol that represents a brand or its company

marketing   all the business activities that present a product, its brand, its image, and its reputation to the customer

advertising   a commercial message that appears in a space or time slot that has been paid for by the advertiser

media   all the means of communication that can present an advertisement to the public, such as magazines, newspapers, television, radio, and billboards

public relations   a marketing effort that tries to put a company and brand name in view of the public without actually buying space or time slots

Interacting with Customers

When you have a good customer-first attitude, you try to view your products from the customer's point of view. When you present a product to a customer, you emphasize the ways the product will satisfy the customer's needs. If you're helping a plumber buy plumbing supplies, for example, you will probably want to emphasize the product's reputation for durability rather than its attractive design. If you're selling bathroom fixtures to an interior decorator, you will want to emphasize attractive design rather than price.

The Customer's Perspective. As you interact with customers, you will help them by figuring out their needs, telling them how your product will satisfy those needs, and demonstrating how you and your company are the best providers of that product.

How to Interact with Customers

When you interact with customers, you should

- Represent your company.
- Try to understand the customer's needs.
- Help the customer see how your company can satisfy those needs.
- Give your customer every reason to return for more business.

1. **Represent your company.** Your friendliness and helpfulness mean that your company is friendly and helpful. Your professional appearance means that your company produces a good product. Your informative presentation means that your company wants to help its customers.
2. **Understand the customer's need.** The best way to find out what your customer needs is to ask. The best questions are **open-ended questions** that cannot be answered with a simple yes or no. "Can I help you?" is likely to bring a response of "No, thanks. Just looking." But "How can I help you?" calls for a more useful answer, like: "I need a party dress for a little girl." You then can go on to ask more questions to find out exactly what the customer needs (see Figure 3.2).
3. **Help the customer see how you can satisfy his or her needs.** When you present your product to the customer, focus on how it can satisfy the needs that your questions have uncovered. If the customer has expressed a need for, say, a lightweight, quiet chainsaw, you can suggest an electric model, emphasizing its weight and quietness rather than its power or warranty.
4. **See objections as needs.** Objections are a customer's reasons for not wanting a given product. You should view objections as *additional needs*. If the customer says, "It's too expensive," the customer needs a lower price, a less expensive model, or easier payment terms. If the customer says, "It's too slow," offer a faster model, or explain why slower is better.

Reading and Study Tips

Main Ideas

The main idea of a paragraph is often stated in the topic sentence, which is usually the first sentence. Take notes by listing the main idea of each paragraph.

open-ended questions questions that cannot be answered with a simple yes or no

❝ *The job can't be finished—only improved to please the customer.* ❞

W. Edwards Deming

Figure 3.2 *The Sales Interaction Cycle*

You want to...	so you say...	and the customer might say...
Learn the customer's needs	"How can I help you?"	"I need an office copier."
Learn more specific needs	"How many copies do you make in a week?"	"Oh, about fifty."
Satisfy the customer's needs	"This copier can handle that load easily."	"No good. It only makes three copies a minute."
Counter the objection by offering a solution	"This model costs a little more, but it's faster."	"But it's way too expensive."
Counter the objection by offering a solution	"You can charge it on our store charge card."	"But I don't have a card."
Counter the objection by offering a solution	"We can issue you one immediately."	"Great! I'll buy it."
Thank the customer	"Thank you very much."	"You're welcome. I appreciate your help."
Give the customer a reason to come back	"Come back and use your card any time. We always have the toner cartridges you need."	"I'm sure I'll be back."

Thinking Critically Many customers say "I'm just looking." *What could you say to start an interaction with the customer?*

Pace Points

Eye Contact
Nothing says "I'm paying attention to you" like looking someone in the eye. One trick to remind yourself about eye contact is to find out the person's eye color.

5. **Thank the customer.** Let the customer know you appreciate the business. Even if the customer does not buy anything, thank him or her for "stopping in."
6. **Give the customer a reason to come back.** Your friendly, helpful attitude will encourage customers to come back again—so will a hint at other services or products you can provide. Remember: Your relationship with the customer does not end when the product is sold. If the customer experiences a problem with the product, do everything you can to resolve the issue. Even if the customer doesn't buy your product, give him or her reason to consider your product in the future.

The Customer-First Attitude

Interacting with customers is easier if you have the right attitude. The sales interaction cycle in Figure 3.2 takes you step by step through the process. You aren't there to sell customers something; you're there to help them buy. All you have to do is match up their needs with your products.

Business-to-Business Customers

business-to-business (B2B) the marketing of products to a company rather than to an individual or retail customer

Jake and Laura interact with retail customers. At some point in your career, you will probably have to interact with business customers—that is, a company rather than an individual. This is called **business-to-business** (or **B2B**) customer interaction.

Figure 3.3 *Customer Problems and Solutions*

Problem	• Delay in reaching a person	• Staff fails to solve the customer's problem	• Customer didn't like treatment
Possible Causes	• Not enough phone lines • Not enough staff • Other complaints not handled fast enough • Too many complaints	• Untrained staff • No resources for solution • Inadequate problem-solving process • Company offers no solution	• Staff has poor attitude • Poor phone skills • Inefficient process
Possible Solutions	• More phone lines • More staff • Better training for staff • Better complaint handling process • Prevention of the causes of complaints	• Better staff training program • Easier staff access to resources • Revision of the problem-solving process • Creation of new solutions	• Training all staff or the individual responsible • Streamlining the process • Discussing the problem and possible solutions with staff

Thinking Critically Here are the main pitfalls of handling customer complaints and problems by phone. *Can you think of any different problems? How would you handle them?*

A Different Kind of Customer

The business customer is a bit different from the retail customer. The business customer isn't buying what he or she wants, but rather what his or her company wants. This means

- The buying decision will be based on real needs, rather than psychological desires.
- The objective of the decision maker isn't to own the product, but rather to succeed in business.
- The decision maker will have to justify the decision to the person to whom he or she reports.
- You may not be able to talk with the actual decision maker.

As you deal with these differences, the most important rule of customer interaction still applies: The customer comes first.

The Same Principles

The principles of business-to-business customer interaction are essentially the same as those of the retail situation, but a little more intense:

1. **Be professional.** Your dress and grooming have to meet professional rather than general fashion standards.
2. **Understand what the customer needs.** Business customers tend to be very specific in their needs and are usually very open about explaining them. One need is often left unsaid: the need for a product to perform well so the buyer's business runs smoothly. Large projects—the leasing of a fleet of trucks, the installation of an office telephone system, the development of specialized software—may demand an equally large effort by a team of your colleagues. The team will need to plan the research effort, and you will need to play your part on the team.

3. **Help the customer see how you can satisfy needs.** The business customer will probably be less influenced by advertising and more demanding of comprehensive technical information. You'll probably need to put things in writing, and those words may be legally binding. Be logical, organized, complete, and accurate in what you promise. If you can't talk to the decision maker, be sure the person you talk to can present your information well.
4. **See objections as needs.** Try to foresee objections and counter them before they're made.
5. **Give the customer reason to come back.** Thank the customer. Deliver more than you promised. Follow up. Foresee future needs. Make sure your company backs its promises and its products.

Cultivating Customer Loyalty and Respect

Your customers want good products, and you want good customers. Good customers feel a certain loyalty to the companies that have served them well in the past. Sometimes that loyalty is directed at the person who has helped them.

Customer loyalty is founded on

- Good service from the people who represent the company.
- Good service from the products the customer bought.
- Good customer service experiences after the sale.

Nurture Loyalty

Loyal customers come back for more. They tend to want your product even before you tell them about it. They also tend to tell other people about your product and your company, and maybe even about you. So developing loyalty in a customer is as important as all the marketing your company does to attract new customers.

Do what you can to nurture loyalty in your customers.

- Thank them for their business.
- If possible, contact them to see if they have been served well by you and your product.
- Make every effort to handle complaints and solve any problems that come up.
- Follow up to make sure the solutions worked.
- Keep customers advised of new products and opportunities.

Let's Do Lunch

A good business customer is worth a good business lunch. As you learned in Chapter 2, a meal is a good opportunity to get to know a customer better and learn how your company can help his or her company. It also may be a good time to talk a bit about a new product or opportunity. Of course, a meal shared is a good way to build customer loyalty. Just make sure you pick up the tab!

No Sale

Sometimes customers just can't be satisfied. You do your best to figure out what they need and to explain how your product can satisfy those needs, but for some reason, they don't buy. Apply two strategies to focus on solving a potential problem.

Tips From a Mentor

Ten Things Customers Want When Shopping

- **A smile.** Even if you are on the phone, a customer can hear in your voice when you are smiling.

- **A pleasant and cheerful manner.** Your smile may be the first impression, but a positive, upbeat attitude will leave a lasting impression!

- **VIP treatment.** No matter what service the person wants, treat him or her like your most important customer—because for that moment, he or she is! Remember, a valued customer may become a loyal customer.

- **Speed and efficiency.** Be sensitive to time issues. Never rush customers, but don't ramble on or let yourself be distracted from serving them.

- **Honesty.** Admit a mistake. Don't promise something you can't deliver. If you can't help a customer, don't fake it—find someone who can help.

- **Your full attention.** Don't take other calls, join other conversations, or otherwise let yourself be diverted from helping your current customer.

- **Professional courtesy.** Be polite. Act comfortably, but not informally with customers. Don't use their first names without asking their permission. Find the middle ground between businesslike and friendly.

- **Expertise.** Know your business and stay informed about happenings around your company. Keep updated on products, displays, specials, and changes in your industry.

- **A good listener.** Everyone needs to be heard. Sometimes customers need to vent—don't interrupt, even if you disagree with what the customer is saying. Obvious exceptions would be if a patron is cursing, insulting you, or disturbing other customers.

- **Follow up.** Make sure the customer gets what he or she needs and is satisfied. If you asked someone else to help the customer, check back to see that he or she was helped.

1. **Find out what went wrong.** Consider these questions: Was the product completely inappropriate for the customer's needs? Does the customer have a bad impression of your company or its products? Did something go wrong in the delivery, installation, or service process? Did the marketing message reach the customer? Was your sales presentation weak? Maybe the customer can give you answers. Maybe you and your team should sit down and try to figure things out.
2. **Correct the problem.** If you don't correct the problem, you'll probably have similar poor results next time you present the product to a customer. If the problem was price, find a way to lower it. If the problem was reputation, focus your next presentation on improving that reputation.

Pace Points

Smile, Everyone!
Remind employees to smile by putting up a mirror where only they can see it. Hang it by a door going into the public area.

The Cost of Mistakes

Mistakes can reach customers in many ways—as defective products, as delivery of the wrong product, as errors in invoices, as unintended insults, as excessive pressure to buy, as failure to resolve problems correctly, and so on. Mistakes mean more than wasted materials or wasted time. They can cause loyal customers to stop buying or even defect to the competition. When that happens . . .

- Marketing efforts that attracted the customer were wasted.
- The ex-customer will discourage other potential customers.
- Current sales revenues dip.
- Future sales revenues dip.
- Preparation for future sales was wasted effort.
- The effort you put into your customer relationship was wasted.
- The customer's defection weakens your company while strengthening the competition.
- The mistake and the defection hurt morale at your company.

No matter how much pressure you are under, no matter how much work you have to do, slow down enough to do the job right.

QUICK RECAP 3.3

INTERACTING WITH CUSTOMERS

- You represent your company, so look professional and be as helpful as you can.
- Learn the customer's needs.
- Show the customer how your product can satisfy a given need.
- Give your customer a reason to come back.
- Keep that customer-first attitude.
- Business customers have very specific needs.
- On big projects, work with your team to help the customer.
- Nurture loyalty in your customers so they come back to do more business.
- When customers choose not to buy, find out why and try to solve the problem.

CHECK YOURSELF

1. What are the main steps in the sales interaction cycle?
2. How can you nurture customer loyalty?

Check your answers online at **www.mhhe.com/pace.**

BUSINESS VOCABULARY

open-ended questions   questions that cannot be answered with a simple yes or no
business-to-business (B2B)   the marketing of products to a company rather than to an individual or retail customer

Managing Customer Complaints

It's bound to happen: You make a promise and deliver the product, but something goes wrong. The product has a defect. Or delivery is delayed. Or the wrong product is delivered. Or the invoice is wrong. Or it isn't what the customer wanted. Or the customer can't figure out how to assemble it.

The Customer's Problem Is Your Problem. The customer comes first, so when the customer comes back, you need to set things straight. Don't just take care of the product; prove to the customer that you are still there to satisfy needs. In this section, you'll learn how to approach complaints as opportunities to strengthen customer relations.

Customer Service

It's normal for customers to have questions about what they bought or even complaints about **product quality** (how well the product was made) or **product performance** (how well the product does what it's supposed to do). It is essential that someone in your company resolve these issues in a positive and constructive manner. This process is called customer support or *customer service*.

Whether you are selling, helping customers with their problems, or managing the people who help the customers, you should understand how to use complaints as opportunities.

Complaints Are Opportunities

Be glad when your customers complain! At least they didn't throw your product in the trash and go look for another company's product. At least they demonstrated a hope that your company cares about the satisfaction of its customers.

Every customer complaint is an opportunity to

- Serve the customer.
- Prove your concern for your customer's satisfaction.
- Learn about problems with your product.
- Learn what other customers may be thinking about your product.
- Continue an ongoing relationship with the customer.
- Give the customer a reason to continue doing business with you.

Solve the Problem

Handling complaints is a lot like selling a product. Instead of helping a customer by identifying a need and satisfying it, you will help by identifying a problem and resolving it. To resolve a problem is to find a solution that satisfies the customer. It is

product quality how well the product was made and how free of defects it is

product performance how well a product does what it's supposed to do

very important that you resolve a customer's problem. Here are eight steps to follow for every customer complaint.

1. **Start by apologizing.** Tell the customer that you're sorry he or she has had a problem with your product.
2. **Indicate that you want to resolve the problem.** Tell the customer you will do everything you can to help. This will do much to calm them and encourage their cooperation.
3. **Identify the problem.** Ask questions until you fully understand what went wrong. Was it a defective product? If the customer is dissatisfied with performance, how so and what had he or she expected? Is the problem one of knowing how to use the product?
4. **Resolve the problem.** Your company probably gives you several options for resolving complaints. Do not offer a solution you are not authorized to make. Do not resolve the wrong problem, such as replacing a product when the real problem was a customer not knowing how to use the product. If you can't resolve the problem, pass it on to someone who can.
5. **Apologize for an inconvenient solution.** If the solution is an inconvenience, such as sending the product to the company for repair, admit it and apologize. Minimize the inconvenience if you can. Emphasize that you will do everything you can to expedite the resolution.
6. **Document the incident.** Keep a detailed record of who called, when, how the customer perceived the problem, how you identified the problem, all the solutions you offered, the solution the customer accepted, and whether the customer was satisfied.
7. **Follow up.** Follow up on the resolution of the problem by contacting the customer to verify that the solution worked. See if there's anything else you can do to guarantee customer satisfaction with the solution, the product, and the company.
8. **Prevent further problems.** How can your company prevent repetitions of the problem that caused the complaint? Once the problem has been identified, it needs to be communicated to the person who can fix the cause.

Prepare for Problems

The process for resolving complaints demands quite a bit of preparation. The person who handles complaints must know

- What questions and complaints to expect.
- Available solutions for the expected complaints.
- How to handle angry customers.
- Answers to expected questions.
- Procedures for specific solutions, such as returning products.
- The complaint-handling process, including reporting and following up.

On Hold

Your Challenge

You are a customer service representative for a large business. A customer calls about an error on his bill. Your entire department had gone to lunch together, so the customer has been kept on hold for 15 minutes. You know that the accounting department has the information needed to help the customer, but you sense that the customer will not allow you to put him on hold again. What do you do?

The Possibilities

A. Apologize for the wait and explain that everyone had been to lunch. Then transfer the call to accounting.

B. Tell the customer that he may not have had to wait if he had called the correct department, then transfer him to accounting.

C. Apologize for the wait and try to access the accounting files yourself.

D. Apologize for the wait and then explain that only accounting has the information he needs. Give him the choice of being transferred to accounting or having someone from accounting call him back that afternoon.

Your Solution

Choose the solution that you think will be most effective and write a few sentences explaining your opinion on a separate sheet of paper. Then check your answer with the answer on our Web site: **www.mhhe.com/pace**.

Pace ONLINE

Managing Customer Service

Taking care of customer questions, complaints, and problems is key to any company's success. If you yourself will be helping customers, prepare yourself. Know the answers, procedures, and the process.

If you demonstrate your concern for customers with problems, you may soon find yourself managing the people who deal with the customers. These people will depend on you to

- Impress them with the importance of a customer-first attitude.
- Outline the foreseeable problems and complaints.
- Train them in the process of handling problems.
- Help them when they can't solve problems.

Help Desks and Tech Support

If you've ever called a help desk, call center, or technical support line, you probably know how the experience can be good or bad. You may get a busy signal several times, then have to punch in an endless series of numbers to get to the right department. You may get put on hold for 20 minutes or more, only to get cut off or told that your problem can't be solved.

If you've ever been through that, you can imagine how customers feel when dialing up your company's help desk or tech support line. They are tremendously relieved to hear an actual human being pick up the phone on the first ring, a person who proceeds to do everything necessary to solve their problem. The quality of assistance that customers receive over the phone is almost as important as the quality of the product they bought. Your can ensure quality assistance over the telephone by following a few basic rules:

1. **Be human.** Doing business by phone reduces the closeness of person-to-person contact. It is therefore all the more important to be warm, friendly, and sincere when helping someone by phone.
2. **Tune in to tone of voice.** Since callers cannot see facial expressions, eye contact, or body language, they tend to rely on tone of voice to interpret what they hear. You should pay special attention to the way they speak. You should strive to sound both friendly and professional.
3. **Be responsive.** As the caller explains the problem, respond with brief, positive words, such as *Yes* and *That's interesting.* This will remind the caller that you are paying attention.
4. **Own your customer.** To own your customer is to stick with the customer until all problems are resolved, even if the customer is transferred to another employee or department. Ask the caller's name and phone number. Be sure the caller knows your name and phone number. The person who owns the customer should follow up to make sure the problem has really been taken care of.

Track problems

If you are supervising the people who handle customer problems and complaints, your job is to watch the whole process. You want to see trends and opportunities for improvement: Keep your eye on the big picture.

Track Customer Problems   Recurring problems are big problems. The best way to spot (and then correct) recurring problems is to track them. Personnel who handle customer complaints should keep records, and management should review them to look for patterns. A standardized problem report form will make it easier for you to review the problems your personnel solved (or failed to solve).

Track Customer Service Problems   Your customer support process should undergo continuous improvement. Customer service personnel should work with management to identify problems they have in helping customers.

Hold Customer Service Staff Meetings   Hold periodic meetings with customer support staff so they can discuss common customer problems, new solutions, and problems solving customer problems. You also can use these meetings to reinforce the importance of your company's customer-first approach.

Manage from the Middle

If you are supervising the staff who handle incoming customer calls, you have to be reaching out in two directions: to staff and to management.

New Attitudes / New Opportunities

Meet Arianne Milano. Arianne works as operations manager for Saddleback Educational, direct mail catalogue distributors of educational books, materials, and software. As a manager for a company that depends on its customer, she understands the importance of customer relations. Here's what she has to say about . . .

The Most Important Concept to Understand About Customer Service "Customer service is a link between the customer and the company. To the customer, the customer service representative IS the company. In many cases, this is the only person that the customer will ever speak to. It's especially true in a direct mail marketing company like ours."

The Importance of Understanding Your Customer "It's very important to understand who you are speaking with, who the end user of your product is, and who the purchaser is so that you can serve each one better. We have an unusual situation, because our end user is not the customer. Our customer is often a teacher and our end user is a student. So for us, the customer service department has to understand that when they are speaking to a teacher, they are really trying to service both a teacher and a student. The retail industry approaches customer service differently because the end user is the person that you are speaking to. It's a little easier to understand your customer."

What Employees with No Experience in Customer Service Should Keep in Mind "Everyone has purchased something in his or her life, so we are all customers. When you are on the phone or face-to-face with a customer, you have to remember that point of view. Think about what you want and expect as a customer, and give the same respect and patience to your customer. When searching for people to fill these positions, we look for someone who is very patient and friendly, and who understands that we are all customers."

The Old Adage that the Customer is Always Right "The customer is always right in any industry because if it wasn't for the customer, the industry would not exist! Try to find a balance where both the customer and the company are happy. Sometimes it's difficult, but it's worth it to keep a customer. In the grand scheme of things, it's usually not worth arguing your point. Don't waste time and money on a small problem that's not worth it, and that customer will hopefully return—and tell others about your excellent service."

Communicate with Staff The people who talk with customers are the people who know where the problems are. They know what customers are complaining about. They know the difficulties in solving those problems.

Communicate with Management You are the bridge between the frontline staff who interact with customers and the management that has the capability to solve problems within the company. First and foremost, management needs to know when there are problems with the products. Management also needs to know whether staff require more training, whether the phone technology is working right, and whether staff have ready access to the resources they need to solve problems. Your job is to monitor and analyze phone staff reports and then inform management of problems and possible solutions.

Monitor Customer Service Personnel

To see if your people are helping your customers as efficiently as possible, you should monitor their performance. It is quite appropriate for a supervisor to listen in on help desk and tech support calls. (Personnel and customers should be aware that calls may be monitored.) You want to listen in to see if personnel

- Try to solve the problem.
- Succeed in solving the problem.
- Use a positive tone of voice.
- Follow correct procedures.
- Are polite, friendly, and helpful.

QUICK RECAP 3.4

MANAGING CUSTOMER COMPLAINTS

- Use complaints as opportunities to detect product problems, monitor customer satisfaction, and impress customers with your company's commitment.
- Complaints are problems to be solved. Solve them.
- Prepare yourself to handle complaints by knowing what to expect and where to find solutions.
- If you supervise people who handle customer complaints, be sure they are trained.
- When handling complaints by phone, make extra effort to sound human, friendly, and responsive.
- If you are at a supervisory or management level, track and analyze customer complaints, and track your company's success in dealing with them.
- Your staff can probably identify difficulties in helping customers and suggest improvements.
- Be sure that the management above you knows what's happening at the front line where your company interacts with customers.
- Monitor customer service staff to see who needs help serving customers better.

CHECK YOURSELF

1. How can you use customer complaints as opportunities?
2. List eight steps you should take as you help customers solve their problems.

Check your answers online at **www.mhhe.com/pace.** *Pace* ONLINE

BUSINESS VOCABULARY

product quality   how well a product was made and how free of defects it is
product performance   how well a product does what it is supposed to do

The customers who pay money for your company's products and services are **external customers.** But as a member of your company team, you may work in a supportive role—one in which you have no contact with external customers. Instead, you are serving internal customers—people in your company who need what you do or make as part of your job. Likewise, you have internal suppliers—people who provide you with what you need to do your job.

Internal Customers are Your Link to External Customers. By serving your internal customers well, you serve the customers who buy your company's products. Your approach to these two kinds of customers should be basically the same, with a few crucial exceptions. In this section, you will learn how to satisfy the needs of your internal customers.

Internal Customers

Internal customers are people within your company who need the services of others in the company. For example, since you need your paycheck, you are a customer of the payroll department. Since everyone in your company works with and depends on someone else, and everyone serves someone else, everyone in your company is both a customer and a supplier.

Companies often recognize themselves as systems of internal customers and suppliers, and they expect their employees to work with each other as such. In other words, your customer-first attitude should extend to the people in your company. To find who your internal customers are, see Figure 3.4.

Serve Internal Customers Well

Everything you learn about serving customers applies to internal customers. You should find out who your internal customers are and what they need. Then, you should satisfy those needs and work to make internal customers glad they are working with you. View internal customers as your link to the paying customers.

You can do this by

- Communicating with them.
- Foreseeing their needs.
- Avoiding mistakes.
- Treating them with respect.

Internal customers are your link to external customers—the ones who buy your company's products and, ultimately, pay your salary.

Identifying Your Internal Customers

You can start to identify your internal customers even before you begin your new job. How? During your job interview, ask who your internal customers will be. The

---

Reading and Study Tips

Figures

Figures are simply a different way to organize text. Read the title and headings to help you know what the figure is about and how to read it.

external customers the customers who pay money for your company's products and services

internal customer someone in a company who needs the products or services provided by someone else in the company (an internal supplier)

Figure 3.4 *Internal Customers*

Department	Product	Internal Customers
Payroll	Paychecks (accurate and on-time)	Company's employees
Accounting	Accurate financial information	Company's management and investors
Marketing	Information (advertising, packaging, etc.) for potential buyers	Sales representatives, distributors, product managers, etc.
Warehouse	Delivery of the ordered products to the shipping department	Shipping department
Maintenance	Company buildings, machines, and other assets in clean, safe, and working order	People who use your company's facility
Information Technology	Complete, accurate, timely information and service	Everyone who uses information or computer systems

Thinking Critically Brainstorm a list of other people or departments in a company. *Who are their internal customers?*

question itself makes you sound knowledgeable and concerned. When you start a new job, the company may provide you with a list of your internal customers, but you'll also need to do some thinking to identify them all. Watch for people who

- Talk with you by phone.
- Send you memos or receive yours.
- Give you assignments.
- Depend on your work.
- Are part of your team or department.

Don't Forget Your Internal Suppliers

internal suppliers People in a company who provide something to other people in the company (internal customers)

Identifying **internal suppliers** involves basically the same process as identifying internal customers. Look for the people with whom you communicate, people you depend on for products or information, and members of your team.

Communication

It is essential that you maintain communication with your internal customers and suppliers. Study these suggestions and sample communications:

1. Develop a rapport (a comfortable, trusting, conversational relationship) with customers so that communications run smoothly. Let them know that you recognize them as internal customers and that you are working to help them.
   - *Example:* You might simply say over lunch, "If we don't get the right items over to your department in time, you tell me, okay? I'll make sure it doesn't happen again."

2. Ask customers what they need and tell them what you can offer.
   - *Example:* A manager may say to one of his supervisors, "What can I do to make your life easier?" The supervisor replies, "It would be good to receive a daily list of new orders." Then the manager offers, "Better yet, I'll e-mail a list of orders twice a day."
3. Tell suppliers what you need and ask them what they can offer.
   - *Example:* "I need this whole report put into a PowerPoint program. Can you get it to me by Thursday?"
4. Keep the communication going two ways so that your customers know what you are doing, and you know what they are doing.
   - *Example:*

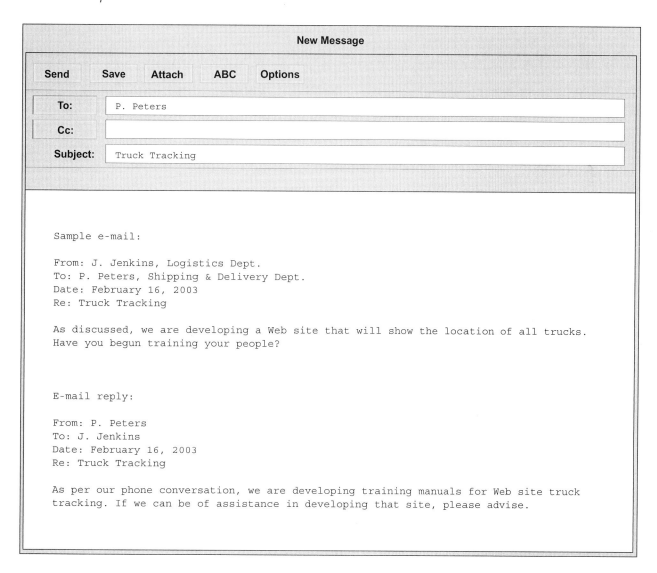

5. Watch for signs of poor communication such as delivery errors, missed meetings, requests for clarifications, and lost documents or e-mail.
   - *Example:* A manager may say to himself, "Uh-oh. Something's wrong. That's the third time he misunderstood me. I'd better figure out the problem."

6. Eliminate obstacles to communication such as busy phone lines, slow office mail, poor handwriting on order forms, information incorrectly relayed, and so on.
   - *Example:* You may leave a message on your supervisor's voice mail, "Jack, this phone tag isn't working, so I think it's better if I update you by e-mail. Does that work for you? Please let me know."

7. Bridge gaps in communication; that is, information that doesn't make it all the way to the internal customer, perhaps because of travel schedules, poorly run meetings, poorly designed order forms, poor writing skills, and so on.
   - *Example:* You may end a meeting by saying, "Just in case you didn't catch everything I said, I'm going to leave you with a list of who's to do what."

8. Improve communication constantly by improving writing skills, planning meetings and presentations better, encouraging others to communicate, tracking down the sources of errors, and making phone calls and e-mails more effective.
   - *Example:*

Mail

New Message

Send | Save Draft | Attach | Tools | Cancel

To:

Cc:

Bcc:

Subject:

```
Sample e-mail:

To: All Marketing Personnel
Re: Improved Communications

To prevent future problems with conflicting travel schedules, I'd like to suggest you
e-mail all travel schedules to me daily. Please call with any questions. I can be
reached at extension 43.
```

See typical internal customer–supplier communication problems in Figure 3.5 for more examples.

Figure 3.5 *Typical Internal Customer-Supplier Communication Problems*

Problem	Possible Cause	Possible Solution
Warehouse sends wrong product to shipping department	Poor handwriting on order form	Type orders or use forms that don't depend on handwriting
Team member misses meeting	She didn't read e-mail memo about meeting	Code e-mail for importance or request confirmation of receipt
Team members don't follow through on meeting decisions	Decisions and assignments were not made clear at meeting	Confirm decisions and assignments in written meeting report
Customer always asking what you meant by your last e-mail	Poor organization in expression of your thoughts	Plan what you are going to write, then re-read with an eye for clarity
Your assistant sends the wrong documents to your client	Your instructions were unclear	Put instructions in writing or be more specific in your instructions
Internal customer–supplier meeting accomplishes nothing	No one informed of objectives beforehand	Inform everyone of meeting's objectives so they can prepare

Thinking Critically Problems have causes and solutions. *Think of a problem, cause, and solution you have confronted at home or at work.*

Increased Efficiency, Reduced Costs

All companies want to increase efficiency and reduce costs. To **increase efficiency** means to accomplish things in less time, with less effort, or with fewer errors. To **reduce costs** means to reduce the actual spending of money, as well as to reduce the time it takes to perform tasks and eliminate needless tasks.

The internal customer–supplier relationship is an excellent place to look for ways to increase efficiency and reduce costs. Talk with your customers and suppliers to see where you can streamline processes and cut waste.

increase efficiency to accomplish things in less time, with less effort, or with fewer errors

reduce costs to reduce the actual spending of money, as well as to reduce the time it takes to perform tasks and eliminate needless tasks

Identify Needs

You need to know what your customers need. Sometimes they will tell you; sometimes you will have to ask. Sometimes you just have to tell them what you can offer. Rapport with your customers will do much to help you identify needs that you can satisfy. Talk with them. Meet with them. Discuss their needs and how those needs are changing and figure out how you can offer them more.

Some needs go without saying: the need for promptness, accuracy, correctness, confirmation, recognition, respect, and so on. Don't wait to be told these things. Think a little about what else your customer might need, and then do it.

Dr. Joe Pace
QUALITY

"Quality is a person's showcase—it is the work we do. As in nature, we should strive for perfection."

Foresee Needs

As you get to know your internal customers better, you'll be able to foresee their needs. If you know what they want, don't wait for them to ask. If you're not sure, ask them. Sometimes you may be able to foresee a need before your customers see it! They will appreciate your suggestion. It indicates that you really are concerned with their needs.

Satisfy Needs

Your internal customers deserve the same customer-first attitude as external customers. In fact, your job description—the specific requirements of your job—is all about the customers you are supposed to help and what you're supposed to do for them.

Your company has probably established some kind of process—a set of standard procedures—that aims at satisfying your internal customer. When you start a new job, one of your first objectives is to learn that process. As you learn the process and customer needs, you may be able to suggest improvements to the process.

Your customer satisfaction process, however, will have to adapt to the unexpected things that happen during daily business. When the unexpected happens, remember that your job isn't to follow the standard process: it is to satisfy the customer. The process must adapt to that ultimate objective.

Follow Up

Did you do what you were supposed to do? Did the package arrive? Did he read the e-mail you sent? Did she understand your instructions? Did the plan work out? Were there any problems? Does the customer have any suggestions for next time? How can you improve?

These are important questions. You can learn the answers by following up. It's important to confirm whether your customer was satisfied. Knowing that, you can look for ways to improve.

Respect Internal Customers

To keep your internal customers satisfied, show them respect.

- Respect their need to receive what you promised.
- Respect their need for information.
- Respect their need for a cooperative relationship.
- Respect their need to help their internal customers.

Respect Internal Suppliers

To keep internal suppliers working both for and with you, show them respect.

- Respect their efforts to help you.
- Respect their need for information.
- Respect their need for a cooperative relationship.
- Respect their need to help other internal customers.
- Respect their need to know or foresee your needs.
- Respect their need to hear, "Thank you."

Avoid Mistakes

As mentioned earlier in this chapter, mistakes are expensive. Even if the external customer never sees the mistakes or feels their direct effects, mistakes cut down on efficiency and profitability, and they cause stress to the internal supplier–customer

Ten Friendly Phrases for an Internal Customer

- *"How can I help you?"* or "How can I make this right?" invites colleagues to specifically suggest how they want their problems to be solved.

- *"Thank you for bringing this to my attention."* This phrase helps your co-worker know that you want to make things right.

- *"I'm sorry"* or "I apologize for the inconvenience" goes a long way to calm down an angry co-worker.

- *"I can see how you'd feel that way."* The co-worker will feel that you are paying attention to his or her needs.

- *"I don't know, but I would be happy to find out for you."* Be sure to follow through immediately.

- *"Perhaps my manager can help you"* or "I believe the personnel department could fix that." Always emphasize the help that's available, not the fact that you cannot give it.

- *"Let me give you that phone extension number"* is better than "You have to call . . ."

- *"I want to be sure I understand—do you mean . . . .?"* The co-worker will feel that you are listening to him or her, and you will get a better idea of his or her needs.

- *Use the co-worker's name.* Nothing sounds friendlier to a person than his or her own name.

- *"Is this solution acceptable?"* The problem is not really solved if the co-worker isn't satisfied. Be sure he or she is before you end the conversation.

relationship. When you make a mistake, it's usually your internal customer who suffers most.

Mistakes happen. When they happen between you and your internal customer or supplier, the two of you should admit the mistake and figure out what went wrong. There's little excuse for a mistake happening a second time.

QUICK RECAP 3.5

INTERACTING WITH INTERNAL CUSTOMERS AND SUPPLIERS

- Internal customers are the people in your company for whom you provide a service as part of your job.
- You should identify your internal customers and their needs.

- It is important to maintain close and ongoing communication with internal suppliers and customers. Look for ways to improve the communication process.
- Look for ways to reduce cost and increase efficiency in your internal supplier–customer relationships.
- Follow up to confirm that you have provided internal customers with what they need.
- Respect the many needs of internal customers and suppliers.
- Make all necessary efforts to avoid mistakes.

CHECK YOURSELF

1. Who is an internal customer?
2. In what ways are communication between you and internal customers important?

Check your answers online at **www.mhhe.com/pace.**

BUSINESS VOCABULARY

external customers   the customers who pay money for your company's products or services

internal customer   someone in a company who needs the products or services provided by someone else in the company (an internal supplier)

internal suppliers   people in a company who provide something to other people in the company (internal customers)

increase efficiency   to accomplish things in less time, with less effort, or with fewer errors

reduce costs   to reduce the actual spending of money, as well as to reduce the time it takes to perform tasks and eliminate needless tasks

Chapter Summary

3.1 The Importance of the Customer

Objective: *Gain an understanding of what a customer is and how to recognize what customers need and want.*

In this section, you learned that the customer comes first. Customers have needs, and your company's objective is to satisfy a customer need with a product, a service, or both. You also learned how your company's marketing department will analyze customer demographics in order to create advertising and public relations that stimulate the customer's interest in your product. By knowing what your customers are looking for, you can more easily satisfy their needs.

3.2 Understanding Advertising and Public Relations

Objective: *Study the importance of corporate identity, logos, and brand names and how to use these identities to appeal to customer needs, attitudes, and lifestyles.*

In this section you learned how your company uses marketing to build customer recognition of its products. By being aware of product images and brand names, and by monitoring your company's advertising and public relations campaigns, you can better understand what customers expect. You yourself are part of the effort to make your company and its products look good, so customers should see you as helpful, knowledgeable, and professional.

3.3 Interacting with Customers

Objective: *Learn how to use attitude and language to cultivate customer loyalty and respect.*

In this section you learned how to provide customers with what they need. You start by being a worthy representative of your company. Once you know what the customer needs, you can help the customer by explaining how your product satisfies those needs. A positive, let-me-help-you attitude makes this process more productive. In business-to-business interactions, you would consider the needs of both the customer company and the person with whom you deal.

3.4 Managing Customer Complaints

Objective: *Become familiar with the principles of help desks, call centers, and tech support networks and how they are used to help customers.*

Customer complaints are opportunities for you to prove your commitment to them. In this section, you learned the importance of solving customer problems. You solve them by indicating your sincere desire to help, then identifying the problem, resolving it, and, when possible, following up to make sure the customer is satisfied. You also document the incident so your company can track problems. If you manage the people who help customers, make sure they are trained and ready to handle possible complaints.

3.5 Interacting with Internal Customers and Suppliers

Objective: *Understand how the people with whom you work in your company are your customers and suppliers.*

Internal customers and suppliers are people in your company who provide each other with products or services. In this section, you saw that the customer-first attitude includes communicating with internal customers, foreseeing their needs, avoiding mistakes, and treating them with professional respect for their jobs. You learned to focus on reducing costs and increasing efficiency in the customer–supplier relationship.

Business Vocabulary

- advertising (p. 98)
- brand (p. 97)
- business-to-business (B2B) (p. 102)
- commitment (p. 93)
- customer (p. 92)
- demographics (p. 93)
- external customers (p. 113)
- image (p. 97)
- increase efficiency (p. 117)
- internal customer (p. 113)
- internal suppliers (p. 114)
- logo (p. 97)

- marketing (p. 98)
- media (p. 98)
- need (p. 92)
- open-ended questions (p. 101)
- product performance (p. 107)
- product quality (p. 107)
- public relations (p. 98)
- reduce costs (p. 117)
- support (p. 93)
- trade magazine (p. 95)
- trade show (p. 96)
- trademark (p. 97)

Key Concept Review

1. What is a customer? (3.1)
2. When a customer wants to buy a car, what does he or she need besides the actual car? (3.1)
3. What is marketing? (3.2)
4. How does marketing help you help your customers? (3.2)
5. When you interact with a customer, what do you want to learn about him or her? (3.3)
6. How would you describe a good attitude toward customers? (3.3)
7. How are the needs of a business customer different from those of a retail customer? (3.3)
8. How are customer complaints actually opportunities? (3.4)
9. If you manage people who handle customer complaints, how can you help them? (3.4)
10. What are internal customers and suppliers? (3.5)

Online Project

Customer Satisfaction

Use a search engine to find several Web sites that will help you learn how to satisfy customers.

1. What are good keywords and phrases to use with the search engine?
2. Make lists of (a) publications that can teach you more, (b) organizations that help professionals satisfy customers, and (c) events, such as conferences and seminars, that help professionals improve their customer satisfaction performance.

Step Up the *Pace*

CASE A *Solving Customer Problems*

You work for a national trucking company that transports products all over North America. As an account representative, you serve several dozen customers, including grocery product distribution warehouses, a car parts distributor, and a major importer of housewares from China. Recently, several companies have complained of receiving damaged goods. After investigating, you learn that a forklift operator at your central warehouse has been working carelessly.

What to Do

1. Before you identify the cause of the problem, what would you tell these customers? Write a short script of what you might say on the phone.
2. After you have identified the cause of the problem, what would you do? Write a letter to a customer who is threatening to find another shipper.

CASE B *Managing a Call Center*

After six months as a phone operator at the customer call center of a consumer electronics company, you are promoted to supervisor of the call center. A few months later, the vice president of corporate relations says she's been receiving reports of customers who call but don't get the help they need. Some operators are less than polite. Others never really resolve customer complaints. It seems the phones are always busy.

What to Do

1. Write a one-page outline of a plan to improve call-center service. What steps would you take? How would you interact with call-center staff?
2. How would you help the vice president understand the problem and feel confident that it is being resolved?

Forms of Address in Business

How you address someone in business can make the difference between getting an interview and having your résumé thrown into a stack, never to be seen again. Follow the tips below for a letter or a business meeting.

- For mail, such as a cover letter or a memo, use the reader's name and job title. When addressing a woman, use "Ms." unless you know her marital status.
- If a name ends in Ph.D., write "Dr."
- When writing a cover letter, if you don't know the name, call the company to find out! If you cannot get a specific name, write to "Director of Human Resources" and use "Dear Director" in your greeting.
- Even if you know the person informally, never use nicknames when doing business.
- Never use "To Whom It May Concern" or "Dear Sir." These generic phrases are too impersonal for today's business world.
- Ask if you can use someone's first name, unless you already know him or her well.
- E-mail is an acceptable way to communicate in business. Just remember, it should be no more informal than any other business communication!

Which Is Best?

You are writing a thank-you letter to Sara Downing, Associate Director, who has just interviewed you. How would you write her name in the address line?
1. Sara Downing
2. Sara Downing, Associate Director
3. Ms. Sara Downing, Associate Director
4. Ms. Downing, Associate Director

Although none is wrong, the best answer is #3. It gives the most information.

Exercise: On the lines provided, write the greeting you would use in a formal business letter to each person.
1. Elizabeth Martinez

_____

_____

_____

2. Trey Chambers, Ph. D.

_____

_____

_____

3. Mrs. Dana Springer

_____

_____

_____

4. Mila Rossi, CEO

_____

_____

_____

5. Human Resources Director Ryan White

_____

_____

6. Nightshift Manager Dan Abrams

_____

_____

_____

Glossary

A

accounting the business of watching, measuring, and recording the movement of money and other assets

advertising a commercial message that appears in a space or time slot that has been paid for by the advertiser

asset something with value

B

bcc an e-mail feature that sends a "blind copy" of your message to other people without listing their names and addresses

body language body positions and movements that communicate something about you

bond a corporate or government written promise to repay a specific amount in the future

brand a unique name given to a company's product

business-to-business (B2B) sales and service to other businesses that either use the product or service or transform the product into another product; the marketing of products to a company rather than to an individual or retail customer

C

casual day a day when no one wears formal office clothing unless they have an important meeting with people from other companies

casual dress clothes that are slightly less formal than suits

cc an e-mail feature that sends a "carbon copy" of your message to other people, who will know they are receiving a copy

chain of command the ranking or hierarchy of employees that constitutes a system of reporting and supervision that channels information upward and downward through a company

commitment a company's seriousness about delivering what it promises-and more

commodities products regarded as basic goods, such as cotton, oil, coffee, and lumber

communication an exchange of information by speech, in writing, or in subtle ways such as tone of voice, style of clothes, and gestures of respect; the act of moving ideas and information

communication media the ways in which the ideas and information are moved or carried

concierge a hotel employee, usually with a desk in the lobby, whose job is to help guests solve problems and get around town

conference call a phone call that includes people at three or more locations

continuing education education and training pursued after graduation for the sake of better professional performance

customer a person who needs or wants products and services

D

demographics the characteristics of a group of people-their ages, incomes, average incomes for each age bracket, average number of cars per household, and so on

diagnostic services the process of identifying disease and illness

disability a physical or mental condition that limits a person's performance

distribution channel the route that products follow from manufacturing to customers

document to put in writing, noting the date, time, place, circumstances, and people involved

dress code a set of rules that determine how employees should (and should not) dress on the job

E

e-commerce business conducted over the Internet

e-mail written messages that are sent from computer to computer over an office network or the Internet. Typically written as E-*mail, email,* or *e-mail.*

entrepreneurs professionals who assume the risks of new business and lead efforts to improve and expand existing business

etiquette the rules of politeness and courtesy that include table manners, limits of conversation, and other appropriate behavior in public

external customers the customers who pay money for your company's products and services

F

favoritism special treatment or privilege given to an employee for reasons that have nothing to do with work performance

finance the business of acquiring, investing, and managing money

forward an e-mail feature that lets you send someone a message that you have received

G

grooming the preparation of your body for a good professional appearance—everything from haircuts to hygiene

H

harassment the needless or even unconscious tormenting of other people with improper criticism, inappropriate jokes, sexual pressure, ethnic slurs, or humiliation

I

image the idea that the public associates with a product

increase efficiency to accomplish things in less time, with less effort, or with fewer errors

interactive media electronic systems that allow users to input information and receive responses, as in computer games, chat rooms, and computer-based interactive training programs

internal customer(s) people who purchase the products or services of the company for which they work; someone in a company who needs the products or services provided by someone else in the company (an internal supplier)

internal suppliers people in a company who provide something to other people in the company (internal customers)

L

logistics the management of all the details of general distribution

logo a symbol that represents a brand or its company

M

marketing all the business activities that present a product, its brand, its image and its reputation to the customer

media all the means of communication that can present an advertisement to the public, such as magazines, newspapers, television, radio, and billboards

merchandising the planning, developing, and presenting of a company's product lines

N

need in the business sense, everything from outright necessity to realistic desire

network systems links among computers and peripherals that enable several people to share software, files, computers, and peripherals at the same time

O

open-ended questions questions that cannot be answered with a simple yes or no

P

passport a document issued by your own government that identifies you and your nationality

personnel policy a written set of rules and information that pertain to working at a given company

portfolio a collection of an artist's best work

prejudice an attitude toward other people based on nothing more than their race, religion, gender, age, or any other characteristics that have nothing to do with their abilities or behaviors

product performance how well a product does what it's supposed to do

product quality how well the product was made and how free of defects it is

protocol a code of conduct that determines, among other things, how people address each other

public relations a marketing effort that tries to put company and brand name in view of the public without actually buying space or time slots

R

reduce costs to reduce the actual spending of money, as well as to reduce the time it takes to perform tasks and eliminate needless tasks

reply an e-mail feature that sends your response along with the message that you received, reminding the sender of what is being discussed

retailer a business that sells products in small quantities to consumers, often with associated services such as installation and repair

S

sexual harassment (1) any kind of pressure to become intimately or socially involved; (2) exposure to any kind of sexually oriented talk, jokes, messages, pictures, descriptions, humiliation, or references to sexual differences between men and women

stock an investment that gives partial ownership of a company

support a company's efforts to ensure that the customer is satisfied with the product long after it's purchased

T

therapeutic services treatment and therapy for diseases and disorders

trade associations organizations dedicated to improving professional standards in a given industry or profession

trade magazine a publication produced for a particular kind of business rather than for consumers

trade show an event where companies in a given industry present their products or services

trademark a word or phrase that is registered with the government so that no one else can use it

V

virtual office a portable office, consisting mostly of a laptop computer

Visa official permission to enter the country, usually stamped in your passport

voice mail a system that allows a caller to leave a message for a person who does not answer the phone

W

wholesaler a business that buys large volumes of products from manufacturers and sells them to retailers

wire services news organizations that sell articles and photos to the press

G

Gossip, 67, 73
Grooming, 54, 55. *See also* Dress and grooming

H

Harassment, definition of, 64, 69
Headhunters, 5
Health science
    biotechnology, 17
    career cluster, 15–16
    career ladder sample, 18
    definition of, 14
    diagnostic services, 16
    health science workplace, 14
    information and communication services, 16
    jobs, 17–20
    pharmaceutical services, 17
    therapeutic services, 16–17
Help desks, 109
Home health aids, 18
Honesty, 105

I

Image, definition of, 97, 100
Increase efficiency, definition of, 117
Industry trends, 95
Information and communication
    services, 16, 20
Information support and services,
    9–10
Information technology (IT)
    career cluster sample, 11
    definition of, 8
    e-commerce, 10
    information support and services,
        9–10
    interactive media, 10
    IT career cluster, 8–10
    IT workplace, 8
    jobs, 10–13
    network systems, 10
    programming and software development, 10
Insurance services, 36
Insurance underwriters, 38
Interaction with people
    chain of command and, 67–68
    civil rights and, 63–65
    courtesy and, 67
    defending yourself, 64–65
    favoritism, 66
    gossip and, 67
    harassment and, 64, 65–66
    privacy and, 67
    productivity and, 68–69
    respect and, 66–68
    unconscious prejudices, 64

Interactive media, 10, 13
Internal customers
    communication with, 114–117
    customer service and, 113
    definition of, 99, 100, 113
    identification of, 113–114
    marketing and, 99
    needs identification, 117–118
    ten friendly phrases for, 119
Internal suppliers, definition of, 114
Internet
    education and, 6
    information technology and, 8
    job search sites, 16
Interviewing, 49–50
Introductions, 56–61
IT. *See* Information technology

J

Job search
    fastest-growing occupations, 19
    industry research and, 5
    tips for, 5
Journalism, 30, 32

L

Loan officers, 38
Logistics, 23, 27
Logo, definition of, 97, 100

M

Management
    customer service management,
        108–112
    retail/wholesale sales and services and, 24, 25
Marketing, 98–99, 100
Meals. *See* Business meals and travel
Media, definition of, 98, 100
Medical assistants, 19
Medical transcriptionists, 19
Meetings
    dress code for, 51
    planning for, 58–60
Merchandising, 22–23, 27
Mistakes
    avoidance of, 118–119
    in communication, 58–60
    correcting others, 57
    in sales, 105–106

N

Needs, 92–93, 96, 101, 103–104, 117–118
Nelson, Paula, 83
Network administrators, 12